Suppers and Buffets

Suppers and Buffets

By Marguerite Patten

TREASURE PRESS

Frontispiece: CORNISH PASTIES

Acknowledgments

Photographs on pages 19, 37, 41, 44, 49, 52, 53, 61, 65, 72, 73, 81, 85, 89, 93, 103, 115, 119, by John Lee.
Photographs on pages 2, 15, 23, 31, 99, 111, by Syndication International.

First published by Octopus Books Limited

This edition published by Treasure Press
59 Grosvenor Street
London W1

© 1973 Octopus Books Limited

ISBN 0 907407 26 9

Some recipes and illustrations in this
book were originally published in 'Perfect
Cooking' by Marguerite Patten

Printed in Hong Kong

Contents

WEIGHTS AND MEASURES

All measurements in this book are based on Imperial weights and measures.

When a cup measurement is used, this refers to a cup of 8 fl. oz. capacity.

1 Imperial pint=20 fl. oz.

Level spoon measurements are used in all the recipes.

Metric measures: for easy reference

1 kilogramme (1,000 grammes)=2.2 lb

$\frac{1}{2}$ kilogramme (500 grammes)=1 lb (working equivalent)

1 litre=$1\frac{3}{4}$ pints (working equivalent)

$\frac{1}{2}$ litre=1 pint (working equivalent)

Introduction

There are many occasions when a light supper is more suitable than a heavier and more formal meal. If you are in a hurry then it is quicker to prepare – and to eat – a one-dish meal. If you intend to eat informally in the garden or in front of the television screen choose an interesting supper menu that can be served on a tray.

When planning supper menus make sure the meal is as nutritious and well balanced as a dinner – avoid too much bread or pastry, have adequate amounts of protein, vegetables and fruit.

Many of the recipes in this book are planned to be served as part of a buffet meal. One of the most enjoyable and simple methods of entertaining friends is to invite them to a 'help yourself' buffet.

Arrange all the dishes on the table, then relax and let your guests serve themselves. This type of meal means no last-minute 'dishing up' and it creates a pleasantly informal atmosphere. If planning a buffet make sure the food is both easy to serve and to eat with just a fork – cut it into fairly small slices or portions; shred lettuce and other salad greens fairly finely, so they are simple to 'manipulate'. I always try to avoid meat or poultry dishes that contain bones or rather liquid sauces for nothing is more upsetting than to drop food or find it impossible to handle.

When you plan a buffet menu, check that you have a good range of colours on the table. If the meal tends to look a little dull then add interest with colourful garnishes – the pictures in this book show the importance of colour in food.

Do not choose dishes that must be served the moment they are cooked, for it takes time for several people to serve themselves.

You will find ideas under most recipes indicating how that supper dish may be adapted for a party buffet.

One-Dish or Light Meals

If you have had a sustaining mid-day meal you will probably find that one dish alone is sufficient for supper. It is important however, particularly with children, to ensure that this one dish contains an adequate amount of the important foods, in particular protein.

If you choose a satisfying soup for supper this gives adequate protein, providing there is meat, fish or cheese among the ingredients, or you top the soup with grated cheese.

It may well be that on reflecting upon the food served during the day you realize the family has had too little green vegetables or fruit. You may not want the trouble of preparing a green vegetable for supper, so serve grapefruit or other fruits rich in vitamin C (strawberries, blackcurrants, red currants, as well as citrus fruits, provide this vitamin). Raw vegetable salads, particularly those containing shredded cabbage or other green vegetables and tomatoes, are another quick and easy way to give the day's vitamin C, for this cannot be stored in the body, so must be replenished daily.

Individual or family-size pies make an excellent supper dish and raw vegetable salads blend well with these.

If you have had a rather light mid-day meal then your supper dish will need to be more satisfying and the main dishes suggested in this book are easy to digest for a late evening meal as well as being fairly substantial.

In your family you may have your main meal in the evening, in which case serve these dishes for luncheon.

I have suggested where additional courses will turn your one-dish meal into a more interesting one.

SOUPS MAKE A MEAL

The following pages give a few suggestions for satisfying soups. The fish soups, which are served less often than any other, are particularly suitable for a late evening meal.

If you want to turn a ready prepared canned or dehydrated soup into a more substantial meal, simmer diced raw potato, peas or other vegetables in this, diluting the soup with milk. This turns it into a very speedy chowder.

Many soups are delicious topped with grated cheese, cream cheese, cottage cheese or yogurt. Fried croûtons (tiny squares of fried or toasted bread) are an excellent accompaniment to a soup.

Leek and Potato Soup

2 large old potatoes
1 lb. leeks
2 oz. ($\frac{1}{4}$ cup) margarine or butter
1$\frac{1}{2}$ pints (4 cups) white stock or
  water
8 oz. (1$\frac{1}{4}$ cups) shelled peas or
  frozen peas

bouquet garni
sprig mint or pinch dried mint
seasoning
little cream (optional)
Garnish:
paprika

Peel and dice the potatoes. Wash the leeks, cut into rings.
Toss the vegetables in the hot margarine or butter for a few
minutes, take care they do not brown. Reserve a few pieces of
leek for garnish. Add the stock or water, bring to the boil,
simmer for about 15 minutes. Add the peas, herbs and
seasoning.
Continue cooking gently for 30 minutes. Remove the bouquet
garni and either emulsify in a warmed liquidizer or sieve the
soup. Reheat, stir in the cream, if liked. Top with paprika and
the reserved leek slices before serving.
Serves 4–6.

To complete the meal:
This meal lacks protein, but as the soup is very filling, follow
with cottage cheese and fresh fruit.

To serve for a buffet:
Serve in warmed individual soup cups.

LEEK AND POTATO SOUP *(Photograph by RHM Foods Limited)*

Creamed Fish Soup

about 8–12 oz. white fish
1½ pints (4 cups) fish stock
1 oz. cornflour
1–2 oz. butter
seasoning
grated rind 1 lemon

¼ pint (⅔ cup) milk
¼ pint (⅔ cup) thick cream
Garnish:
chopped parsley or dill and/or
   cooked peas
paprika

Put the fish into about ½ pint (1⅓ cups) of the fish stock.
Simmer gently until just tender. Strain the fish from the liquid
and put the stock into a saucepan.
Blend the rest of the fish stock with the cornflour, put into the
saucepan, add the butter, a little more seasoning if required
and the lemon rind. Bring to the boil, cook until slightly
thickened, stirring well. Add the milk and cream and the
flaked fish. Heat for a few minutes only, without boiling. Top
with the garnish and serve.
Serves 4–6.

Variations:
To make a thicker soup, either decrease the amount of fish
stock (which gives a creamier result) or increase the amount of
cornflour to 1½–2 oz. (up to ½ cup).
Creamed shell-fish soup: Use prepared or canned mussels,
shelled prawns or flaked crabmeat instead of white fish.
Slimmers soup: Cook the fish as above. Add to very well
flavoured fish stock and blend in a little yogurt instead of
milk and cream.

To complete the meal:
Serve fresh fruit, as the soup is rich in protein.

To serve for a buffet:
Make sure the fish is finely flaked and serve in warmed
individual soup cups.

Spiced Fish Soup

2 tablespoons oil
1–2 cloves garlic
1 large onion
3 large tomatoes
1½ pints (4 cups) fish stock
½ teaspoon paprika
pinch allspice
good pinch saffron*

pinch turmeric
about 12 oz. white fish
seasoning
Garnish:
croûtons or garlic croûtons
  (see page 112)
parsley

*If using a few saffron strands instead of saffron powder infuse this in the stock for about 30 minutes, then strain and use the stock.

Heat the oil in a pan, fry the crushed garlic, the chopped onion and skinned chopped tomatoes until a thick purée.
Blend the fish stock with all the flavourings, add to the purée, together with the finely diced, skinned raw white fish.
Simmer until the fish is tender. Season to taste and garnish with the croûtons and parsley just before serving.
Serves 4–6.

Variation:
Genoese fish soup: Follow the recipe above and add a few shelled prawns and mussels just before serving.

To complete the meal:
Serve citrus fruit as the soup is rather rich; either grapefruit before the meal or a salad of orange and grapefruit segments after the soup.

To serve for a buffet:
Flake the fish finely and put bowls of croûtons on the table.

Chilled Summer Soup

1 medium-sized lettuce
1 bunch watercress or use a little parsley instead
1 medium-sized bunch spring onions or scallions
1½ oz. butter

1½ pints (4 cups) chicken stock or water and 2 chicken stock cubes
1½ oz. ($\frac{3}{8}$ cup) flour
seasoning
½ pint (1⅓ cups) thin cream
Garnish:
chopped parsley

Wash and shred the lettuce, discard any tough outer leaves. Chop the watercress leaves, or enough parsley to give 1 tablespoon. Chop the white part of the onions together with some of the green stems.

Heat the butter in a saucepan and add the lettuce, watercress or parsley and spring onions. Lower the heat and cook for 10 minutes, stirring several times so the vegetables do not burn. Add most of the stock or water and stock cubes. Simmer gently for 10 minutes, or until the vegetables are tender. Blend the flour with the remaining stock. Add to the soup and cook until thickened. Season well. Sieve or emulsify the soup to give a very smooth purée. If you do this after thickening the soup a skin will not form.

Allow to become really cold, then whisk in most of the cream. Serve in a chilled tureen or soup cups. Top with the rest of the cream and chopped parsley.

Serves 4–6.

Variations:

Use sprigged cauliflower with 1–2 chopped leeks instead of the lettuce, watercress and onions. Sieve or emulsify as above, garnish with paprika.

Use about 6 oz. (2 cups) shredded spinach and spring onions or scallions, but omit the lettuce and watercress. Sieve or emulsify as above, garnish with cream and parsley.

Use a lettuce, ½ peeled chopped cucumber and 1 chopped onion together with the grated rind of 2 oranges. Omit the watercress and spring onions or scallions. Sieve or emulsify as above. Garnish with diced cucumber, serve with quartered oranges.

Chilled 10-Minute Potato Soup

2 tablespoons dehydrated onion
1 pint (2⅔ cups) water
1 or 2 chicken stock cubes
small packet instant potato

shake cayenne pepper
¼ pint (⅔ cup) thin cream
Garnish:
chopped chives and/or parsley

Simmer the onion in the water for a few minutes. Add the stock cubes and dissolve. Stir in the instant potato and blend well. Add pepper. Chill then whisk in the cream. Top with the herbs.
Serves 4–6.

To complete the meal:
Serve a fairly strong flavoured cheese and fruit or fruit salad.

To serve for a buffet:
These are ideal soups as they can be prepared beforehand and chilled. Decorate the edges of soup cups by dipping in lightly whisked egg whites and finely chopped parsley.

Toppings for Soups

A topping for a soup adds not only a garnish but extra food value too; here are some suggested toppings:

Cheese:
Grate Cheddar and other hard cheese; roll cream cheese into small balls; spoon cottage cheese over the hot or cold soup. Crumbled Danish Blue cheese is excellent on vegetable soups.

Sausages:
Slice Frankfurters or cooked sausages and put on vegetable soups.

Nuts:
Blanched almonds make an excellent topping on chilled soups. The almonds may be toasted under the grill to give a contrasting colour.

SEAFOOD

Scampi with Tartare Sauce

24 fresh or defrosted frozen
  scampi (large shrimps)
1 oz. ($\frac{1}{4}$ cup) flour
seasoning

1 egg
2–3 oz. ($\frac{2}{3}$ cup) crisp breadcrumbs
oil or cooking fat for frying

Dry defrosted scampi well. Coat in the flour mixed with seasoning, then in beaten egg and breadcrumbs. Fry in hot oil or fat for 3–4 minutes until crisp and golden brown. Drain on absorbent paper.
Serves 5–6.

Tartare Sauce

$\frac{1}{2}$ pint (1$\frac{1}{3}$ cups) mayonnaise
2 tablespoons chopped gherkins

1–2 tablespoons chopped parsley
1 tablespoon capers

Mix all the ingredients together.
Serves 5–6.

Goujons of Fish
Cut skinned fillets of sole, plaice, whiting or fresh haddock into small strips. Coat and fry as scampi and serve with tartare sauce (above).

Fish in a Jacket

1 lb. frozen puff pastry or puff
pastry made with 8 oz. (2 cups
flour, etc. (see page 20)
4 very large or 6 smaller fillets
white fish
seasoning
Sauce:
1 oz. butter

1 oz. ($\frac{1}{4}$ cup) flour
$\frac{1}{4}$ pint ($\frac{2}{3}$ cup) milk
about 4 oz. (1 cup) mushrooms
Glaze:
1 egg
1 tablespoon water
Garnish:
sliced lemon and parsley

Prepare the pastry and roll out thinly, then cut into 4 or 6
squares, large enough to cover the fish. Lay the fillets flat on a
board, season lightly.
Make a thick sauce with the butter, flour and milk. Add the
chopped uncooked mushrooms and season well. Spread over
half of each fillet. Fold the other half of the fish over the
sauce. Lay on the squares of pastry, moisten the edges, fold
over in triangles and seal the edges. Lift on to a baking sheet,
brush with a little beaten egg, blended with water.
Bake for 10 minutes just above the centre of a very hot oven,
475°F, Gas Mark 8, then lower the heat to moderate,
350–375°F, Gas Mark 4–5 and cook for a further 20–25
minutes until golden brown and well risen. Garnish with
lemon and parsley and serve hot.
Serves 4–6.

Variation:
If preferred, blend flaked cooked fish with a thick sauce and
chopped mushrooms and use as a filling for the pastry.

To complete the meal:
Serve a green salad and fresh fruit.

To serve for a buffet:
Make the pastry into 8–10 smaller squares; fill as the variation
above. Bake for a slightly shorter period.

Puff Pastry

Sieve 8 ounces (2 cups) plain flour and a pinch of salt. Add enough water plus a squeeze of lemon juice to make an elastic dough.

Roll to an oblong shape on a floured board. Place 8 oz. (1 cup) butter in the centre of the pastry dough. Fold the bottom part of the dough over the butter; bring down the top part. Turn, seal the ends and 'rib' the pastry as described under flaky pastry (page 26).

Roll and fold as flaky pastry but allow a total of 7 rollings and 7 foldings and put away between rollings.

Tuna Fingers

Puff pastry (as above)	large can tuna fish
4 tomatoes	1 lemon
seasoning	**Glaze:**
3 hard boiled eggs	1 egg

Roll out the puff pastry until a very thin oblong. Divide into 2 equal-sized pieces. Lift one piece of pastry on to the baking tray.

Slice the tomatoes thinly and put over the pastry, season lightly. Shell and chop the hard boiled eggs. Mix with the well drained flaked tuna fish, the finely grated lemon rind, 2 teaspoons lemon juice and seasoning. Spread over the tomatoes.

Brush the edges of the pastry with water. Cover with the second piece of pastry. Glaze with beaten egg and bake in the centre of a very hot oven, 450–475°F, Gas Mark 7–8 for 15 minutes or until golden and well risen, then lower the heat to very moderate 325°F, Gas Mark 3 and bake for another 10–15 minutes. Serve hot or cold, cut into neat fingers.
Serves 4–6.

Variations:
Use well drained canned or cooked fresh salmon, salmon trout or other white or shell-fish.

Prawn and Cheese Quiche

Pastry
6 oz. (1½ cups) flour, preferably
    plain
pinch salt
3 oz. (⅜ cup) margarine, butter
    or cooking fat
water to mix
Filling:
2 eggs

seasoning
¼ pint (⅔ cup) milk
4 oz. (1 cup) crumbled
    Lancashire cheese
4 oz. (½ cup) shelled chopped
    prawns
Garnish:
few whole prawns
parsley

Sieve the flour and salt, rub in the fat then add sufficient
water to make a firm rolling consistency. Roll out and line a
shallow 8-inch flan ring, sandwich tin or oven-proof baking
dish. Bake 'blind' for about 15 minutes in the centre of a hot
oven, 425–450°F, Gas Mark 6–7, until just set.
Meanwhile beat the eggs with seasoning, add the warmed
milk, cheese and chopped prawns. Pour into the partially
baked pastry case, return to the oven and continue baking in
a moderate oven, 350–375°F, Gas Mark 4–5, for about 25–30
minutes until the filling is firm.
Serve hot or cold garnished with whole prawns and parsley.
Serves 4–5.

Note:
This filling is rather shallow, which means it will set fairly
quickly and is a firm filling, so is ideal to cut and serve for a
buffet. For a less firm filling you can use nearly ½ pint (1⅓ cups)
milk to the 2 eggs for an 8–inch, reasonably shallow, dish.
Allow about 40–45 minutes to set the filling in a very
moderate oven, 325°F, Gas Mark 3.

To complete the meal:
Serve the tuna fingers or quiche with salad.

To serve for a buffet:
Choose the shallow version of the quiche. The tuna fingers
may be cooked then reheated gently.

Prawn and Turbot Salad

1 piece turbot or other white fish, weighing about 6 oz.
seasoning
3–4 oz. (generous $\frac{1}{2}$ cup) shelled prawns
sauce as given in the Fish Cocktail (see page 113) or use mayonnaise with a little lemon juice

1 small green pepper
1 small red pepper
lettuce or watercress
Garnish:
black olives

Poach the fish in well seasoned water until just tender. Do not over-cook for the fish continues to soften as it cools. Cut into small cubes, blend with the prawns.

Prepare the sauce or mix mayonnaise with lemon juice. Add the diced flesh from the peppers (discard the cores and seeds) and the fish.

Put lettuce or watercress on to 4 individual dishes or use scallop shells, as shown in the picture. Spoon the fish mixture on top and garnish with olives.
Serves 4.

Variations:
Use well drained rollmop herrings in place of cooked turbot or other white fish.
Omit the shell-fish and add diced gherkins and/or celery and/or sliced tomatoes.

To complete the meal:
Either serve melon or grapefruit before the salad or fresh fruit after it.

To serve for a buffet:
Use smaller portions as an hors d'oeuvre.

MEAT
AND POULTRY

In addition to the recipes that follow try these ideas for easy
meat and poultry dishes.

Beef in ale:
Mince 1–1¼ lb. good quality cooked beef. Put it into a dish
with 1 grated onion, 1 crushed clove garlic and just under
½ pint (good 1 cup) ale of some kind. Leave to stand for a
short time then heat gently. Add seasoning and a few
tablespoons thick cream and serve with crisp rolls or toast and
a green salad.
Serves 4.

Meat cutlets:
Mince about 12 oz.–1 lb. cooked meat (try a mixture of beef
and ham; lamb and pork; chicken and ham etc.). Mix with a
thick sauce made from 1 oz. butter, margarine or cooking fat,
1 oz. (¼ cup) flour and ¼ pint (⅔ cup) stock. Add 2 oz. (1 cup)
soft breadcrumbs, seasoning and pinch mixed herbs. Cool the
mixture, form into 4 large or 8 small cutlet shapes. Coat in
beaten egg and crisp breadcrumbs and fry until crisp and
golden brown. Drain on absorbent paper. Serve hot or cold
with salad.
Serves 4.

Pork and prune cutlets:
Use lean pork and cook as for Meat Cutlets. Mix about
12 chopped cooked prunes with the mixture. If this seems a
little too soft increase the amount of breadcrumbs slightly.

Fricassée of poultry:
Make a sauce with 1 oz. butter or margarine, 1 oz. (¼ cup)
flour, ¼ pint (⅔ cup) chicken stock and ½ pint (1⅓ cups) milk.

Season this well, add a few sliced fried mushrooms, a few cooked peas or corn and about 1 lb. diced cooked poultry. Heat gently and serve with crisp toast or creamed potatoes.

Sweet and sour cutlets:
Add 2 tablespoons chopped well drained vinegar pickles and 2 tablespoons fairly smooth sweet chutney to the Meat cutlet mixture. Increase the amount of breadcrumbs slightly to compensate for the additional ingredients and chill well before trying to form into cutlets.

Short Crust and Puff Pastry

The ingredients and method for short crust pastry are given fully under the Old English Chicken Pie (page 28). This pastry can be used for many excellent savoury and sweet dishes. Remember if a recipe says 8 oz. pastry it means pastry made with 8 oz. (2 cups) flour, etc., but if buying ready frozen or packet pastry you need to allow the following:
Instead of short crust pastry made with 8 oz. (2 cups) flour, etc. buy or weigh 12 oz. short crust pastry.
Instead of puff pastry made with 8 oz. (2 cups) flour, etc. buy or weigh 1 lb. puff pastry.

Small Savoury Tarts

The following gives about 12 shallow or 8 deeper pastry cases: Make short crust pastry with 6 oz. ($1\frac{1}{2}$ cups) flour, etc. Roll out and line the cases. Spoon the fillings into the uncooked pastry cases and bake for approximately 15 minutes just above the centre of a moderately hot oven, 400°F, Gas Mark 6.
Fillings for uncooked pastry:
Cheese cream tarts: Blend 4 oz. (1 cup) grated Cheddar cheese, 2 eggs, 2 tablespoons thick cream, 2 teaspoons chopped parsley and seasoning.
Fish tarts: Use 4 oz. (1 cup) flaked cooked or canned fish or shell fish instead of cheese.

Fillings for cooked tarts:
Bake the pastry without a filling. Allow 10–12 minutes only towards the top of a hot oven, 400°F, Gas Mark 6. Put in the filling just before serving.

Scrambled egg and sardines:
Mash sardines with a little lemon juice and seasoning. Put into the cases and top with scrambled egg (other cooked fish can be used in place of sardines).

Savoury chicken:
Dice cooked chicken and cucumber, mix with drained canned corn and cottage cheese or mayonnaise. Top with parsley.

Flaky Pastry

8 oz. (2 cups) flour, preferably plain

pinch salt

6 oz. ($\frac{3}{4}$ cup) butter or other fat*

water to mix (as cold as possible)

*A favourite combination is half margarine and half cooking fat.

Sieve the flour and salt into a mixing bowl. Rub in one third of the fat. Add enough water to make an elastic dough.
Roll out to an oblong on a lightly floured board. Divide the remaining fat in half; if hard soften by pressing with a knife. Put over the top two thirds of the pastry in small pieces. Bring up the bottom third of the pastry dough and fold like an envelope. Bring down the top third.
Turn the pastry at right angles, seal the ends of the pastry, then depress this at regular intervals with a lightly floured rolling pin – this is called 'ribbing' the pastry. Roll the dough out into an oblong shape again. If you find it feels sticky and is difficult to roll then put away in a cool place for another 30 minutes, or longer if wished.
Repeat the process described above, using the rest of the fat. Roll out to the required shape, chill until ready to use.
Cook as the individual recipe, but flaky pastry needs a hot to very hot oven to encourage the pastry to rise and to prevent it being greasy. Serve hot or cold.

OLD ENGLISH CHICKEN PIE *(Photograph by RHM Foods Limited)*

Old English Chicken Pie

Short crust pastry:
8 oz. (2 cups) flour, preferably
　plain
pinch salt
4 oz. ($\frac{1}{2}$ cup) fat*
cold water to mix
Filling:
sage and onion stuffing (see
　page 29) or $\frac{1}{2}$–1 packet stuffing
12 oz. (nearly 2 cups) diced raw
　chicken

2 oz. ($\frac{1}{2}$ cup) flour
seasoning
3 sausages (skinless if possible)
2 oz. ($\frac{1}{4}$ cup) butter or cooking fat
$\frac{3}{4}$ pint (2 cups) chicken stock or
　water and 1 chicken stock cube
2 hard boiled eggs
Glaze:
1 egg

*This can be cooking fat, margarine or butter or a mixture of fats.

Sieve the flour and salt. Cut the fat into convenient-sized pieces, drop into the bowl. Rub in with the tips of your fingers until the mixture looks like fine breadcrumbs. Gradually add water to give enough moisture to bind the ingredients together. Use a palette knife to blend. Put on one side while preparing the filling.

Form the stuffing into small balls. Toss the chicken in half the flour, blended with a little seasoning. Halve the sausages. Toss the stuffing balls, coated chicken and sausages in the hot butter or cooking fat until golden brown. Remove from the pan and put into a 2-pint (5–6 cups) pie dish. Stir the remaining flour into any fat remaining in the pan, then gradually add the stock or water and stock cube. Bring to the boil, cook until thickened. Add the coarsely chopped eggs. Pour the sauce over the chicken, stuffing balls and sausages. Cool slightly, then cover with the pastry.

To do this roll out the dough and cut a band of pastry to fit round the moistened edge of the pie dish. Brush the rim of pastry with a very little water. Support the rest of the pastry over the rolling pin. Arrange on top of the pie (slip the rolling pin away). Press the edges together, then cut away the surplus pastry. Decorate the edges by fluting. Make a slit in the centre of the pie to allow the steam to escape. (This encourages the

pastry to crisp.) Decorate with pastry leaves made from the trimmings. Brush with the beaten egg and bake in the centre of a hot oven, 425–450°F, Gas Mark 6–7, for about 20–25 minutes until the pastry is golden brown. Reduce the heat to moderate, 350–375°F, Gas Mark 4–5 and cook for a further 20–25 minutes. Serve hot.
Serves 6.

Sage and Onion Stuffing

Chop 2 medium-sized peeled onions coarsely, simmer in a little salted water. Drain, mix with 1 teaspoon chopped fresh sage or $\frac{1}{4}-\frac{1}{2}$ teaspoon dried sage, 3 oz. ($1\frac{1}{2}$ cups) soft breadcrumbs and 1 oz. melted margarine. Cool, form into balls. If using this recipe for stuffing a joint then double the amount of margarine and moisten the mixture with onion stock or an egg.

To complete the meal:
This is a very satisfying rich supper dish so the ideal accompaniment is a green salad. Choose a refreshing dessert like citrus fruit or lemon sorbet (see page 106).

To serve for a buffet:
Use a little less stock to give a slightly firmer filling. Make very small stuffing balls and dice the chicken and sausages finely.

Steak and Kidney Pie

Filling:
$1\frac{1}{4}$ –$1\frac{1}{2}$ lb. stewing steak
about 8 oz. ox-kidney
nearly 1 oz. ($\frac{1}{4}$ cup) flour
seasoning
1–2 oz. cooking fat

$\frac{3}{4}$ pint (2 cups) stock or water and
  1 beef stock cube
flaky pastry made with 6 oz.
  ($1\frac{1}{2}$ cups) flour etc. (see page 26)
Glaze:
1 egg plus 1 tablespoon water or a
  little milk

Cut the steak and kidney into neat pieces. Blend the flour
and seasoning. Roll the meat in the seasoned flour, fry gently
in the hot cooking fat. Use the higher amount of cooking fat
if the meat is lean. Blend the stock or water and stock cube
into the mixture gradually. Bring to the boil and cook until
thickened. Cover the pan very tightly, cook over a low heat
until almost tender (2–$2\frac{1}{4}$ hours). Make sure the liquid does
not evaporate too much and add more if necessary.
Make the flaky pastry (page 26) while the meat is cooking.
Spoon the meat and a little gravy into a 2–3 pint ($5\frac{1}{3}$ –8 cups)
pie dish, allow to cool; cover with the pastry. Flake the pastry
edges with a knife to encourage it to rise. Make a slit in the
pastry so that the steam escapes during baking and arrange
pastry leaves, made from the trimmings, on top. Beat the egg
with the water. Brush over the pastry to glaze or use milk.
Stand the pie dish on a baking tray, as a precaution in case
any liquid boils out. Bake in the centre of a hot to very hot
oven, 450–475°F, Mark 7–8 for 15–20 minutes. Re-set the
heat to moderate, 350–375°F, Mark 4–5 and cook for a
further 30–35 minutes until the pastry is brown and firm.
Serves 6.
Variations:
Add sliced onions or other vegetables to the steak and kidney.
Use a little red wine in the gravy in place of all stock.
Plate pie: Prepare the steak mixture but use only $1\frac{1}{4}$ lb. meat
and just under $\frac{1}{2}$ pint (generous 1 cup) stock to give a drier
mixture. Double the amount of pastry. Use half to line a
9-inch shallow dish, put in the cooled meat mixture. Cover
with the pastry and bake as the main recipe.

Chunky Pork Supreme

2 onions*
1 lb. lean pork
2 medium-sized carrots
2–3 sticks celery
1 small green pepper (optional)

3 oz. ($\frac{3}{8}$ cup) butter or margarine*
2 oz. ($\frac{1}{2}$ cup) flour*
seasoning
1 pint ($2\frac{2}{3}$ cups) milk
1 bay leaf

Method A
*Omit the onions, 2 oz. ($\frac{1}{4}$ cup) butter or margarine and the flour and use a double packet of onion sauce mix. Prepare the sauce with the milk as the instructions on the packet, then toss the diced pork and vegetables in the 1 oz. butter or margarine and add to the sauce; proceed as Method B.

Method B
Peel and chop the onions, dice the pork, peel and slice the carrots and chop the celery and the green pepper (discard the core and seeds).

Heat all the butter or margarine in the saucepan, fry the prepared vegetables in this for a few minutes. Toss the pork in the flour, blended with seasoning and add to the vegetable mixture. Continue cooking gently until the pork is pale golden coloured. Gradually blend in the milk and stir over a low heat until a smooth thickened sauce. Add the bay leaf. Cover the pan, then simmer gently until the pork is tender, this takes approximately $1\frac{1}{4}$–$1\frac{1}{2}$ hours. Stir occasionally.

Remove bay leaf before serving.

Serves 4–5.

Variations:
Veal suprême: Use diced fillet of veal instead of pork; add the grated rind of 1 lemon to the sauce.

Chicken suprême: Cut a small uncooked frying chicken into small joints (about 8 pieces), use instead of pork.

To complete the meal:
Serve with mixed salad.

To serve for a buffet:
Dice the meat finely, use a little less milk to give a thicker sauce.

CHUNKY PORK SUPREME *(Photograph by RHM Foods Limited)*

Cornish Pasties

Pastry:
1 lb. (4 cups) flour, preferably plain
pinch salt
6–8 oz. ($\frac{3}{4}$–1 cup) fat*
water to mix
Filling:
1 lb. rump steak

2 medium-sized potatoes
2 medium-sized onions
1 small or $\frac{1}{2}$ medium-sized swede (optional)
2 tablespoons stock or water
seasoning
Glaze:
1 egg plus 2 teaspoons water (optional)

Use smaller amount if carrying the pasties on a picnic.

Sieve the flour and salt and rub in the fat. Bind to a rolling consistency with the water.

Cut the meat, peeled potatoes, onions and swede into small neat pieces. If omitting the swede, add a little more potato and onion to give the same amount of filling. Mix with the stock or water and seasoning.

Roll out the pastry and cut round 4 small plates. Put the filling in the centre of each round. Damp the edges of the pastry with water and bring up to form a pasty shape. Flute the edges with your fingers. Lift on to a baking tray. If wishing to give the pastry a good shine blend a beaten egg with water and brush the pasties with this glaze.

Bake for approximately 15–20 minutes in the centre of a hot oven, 425–450°F, Gas Mark 6–7, or until the pastry is golden, then lower the heat to moderate, 350–375°F, Gas Mark 4–5, and cook for a further 20 minutes, or to very moderate, 325–350°F, Gas Mark 3–4, for 25–30 minutes.
Serves 4.

To complete the meal:
Serve green and tomato salads and fresh fruit.

To serve for a buffet:
Make smaller pasties and bake for a slightly shorter period.

Fluffy Topped Bobotee

1–2 medium-sized aubergines
  (eggplants)
1–2 large onions
3–4 large tomatoes
2–2½ tablespoons oil
2 lb. meat from leg of lamb
1 teaspoon curry powder
seasoning
½ pint (1⅓ cups) brown stock
bouquet garni

2–3 tablespoons chopped blanched
  almonds
Topping:
6 tablespoons (½ cup) very smooth
  mashed potato
2 tablespoons thin cream
3 eggs
1–2 tablespoons finely grated
  Parmesan cheese
seasoning

Dice the aubergines (eggplants), the peeled onions and tomatoes and toss in the oil. Dice or mince the lamb and mix with the vegetables. Add the curry powder, seasoning and stock. Simmer for about 15 minutes, stirring well to mix the meat with the vegetables. Transfer to an oven-proof dish, add the bouquet garni and nuts. Cover the dish and cook in the centre of a very moderate oven, 325–350°F, Gas Mark 3–4, for 45 minutes. Remove the bouquet garni.

Mix the potato, cream, egg yolks, cheese and seasoning. Fold in the stiffly whisked egg whites. Spread over the meat and cook for a further 20 minutes.
Serves 5–6.

Variation:
Omit the potato topping and use the traditional savoury egg custard mixture, i.e. beat 2 eggs with seasoning and 12 tablespoons (1 cup) milk. Cook the meat mixture for 45 minutes as the recipe above, remove the bouquet garni. Pour the egg custard mixture over the top of the meat and set for 35 minutes in a very moderate oven.

To complete the meal:
Serve with cauliflower or broccoli. Precede the Bobotee with grapefruit or melon.

To serve for a buffet:
Use the basic recipe.

Lamb Shish-Kebabs with Herbed Sauce

Sauce:
about ½ pint (1⅓ cups) tomato juice
2 teaspoons made mustard
¼ pint (⅔ cup) natural yogurt
shake cayenne pepper
2 teaspoons finely chopped mint
2 teaspoons chopped chives or spring onions
seasoning
¼ teaspoon ground cinnamon

Kebabs:
1 lb. lean lamb (cut from the leg)
1 green pepper
8–12 button mushrooms
4 small tomatoes
12 small cocktail onions
1 oz. butter
seasoning

Mix all the ingredients for the sauce. Put into a shallow dish. Cut the lamb into 1-inch cubes. Put into the sauce and leave for 3–4 hours, turn several times. Lift the meat out of the sauce.

Cut the flesh of the green pepper into 8–12 pieces, discard the core and seeds. Thread the meat and vegetables on to 4 long metal skewers. Brush the vegetables, but not the meat, with the melted butter, season lightly. Cook under a hot grill, turning several times, until tender. Brush the meat once or twice with the sauce. Heat the remaining sauce gently and serve with the kebabs. Serve with boiled rice or crusty bread. **Serves 4.**

Variations:
Sausage kebabs: Use small sausages instead of diced lamb.
Kidney kebabs: Skin and halve lambs' kidneys (use instead of the lamb) and brush with melted butter or add small rolls of bacon to the skewers.

To complete the meal:
Serve with green salad.

Creamed Chicken Curry

$4\frac{1}{2}$ lb. chicken
water
small bunch parsley
seasoning
2 large onions
2 large carrots
Sauce:
2 oz. ($\frac{1}{4}$ cup) butter, margarine or
  chicken fat
2 oz. ($\frac{1}{2}$ cup) flour

1 tablespoon curry powder
$\frac{1}{2}$ pint ($1\frac{1}{3}$ cups) chicken stock
  (see method)
$\frac{1}{2}$ pint ($1\frac{1}{3}$ cups) milk
$\frac{1}{4}$ pint ($\frac{2}{3}$ cup) thin cream
Garnish:
1 green pepper
1 red pepper
cooked rice

Put the chicken into a large saucepan with water to cover, parsley and seasoning. Simmer for 40 minutes. Add the neatly diced onions and carrots and continue cooking until the chicken is just tender. Do not over-cook.

Lift out the chicken, cut into portions. Strain the diced vegetables, put on one side and measure out $\frac{1}{2}$ pint ($1\frac{1}{3}$ cups) stock.

Heat the butter, margarine or chicken fat in the large saucepan, stir in the flour and curry powder, cook for several minutes. Gradually stir in the stock and milk, bring to the boil and cook until thickened, add the joints of chicken, strained onion and carrots. Heat gently.

Lift the chicken on to the hot serving dish, stir the cream into the sauce, season this if necessary. Spoon over the chicken and garnish with rings of peppers (discard cores and seeds) and a border of cooked rice.

Serves 4–6.

Variations:
Use ready cooked pieces of turkey, chicken or pheasant in the sauce.

If a less creamy texture is desired then use 1 pint ($2\frac{2}{3}$ cups) stock and $\frac{1}{4}$ pint ($\frac{2}{3}$ cup) thin cream or milk.

To complete the meal:
A curry like this and the recipe on page 40 is very
sustaining. Follow with a strongly flavoured cheese and
crisp celery or apple.

To serve for a buffet:
The meat balls on page 40 are ideal for a hot buffet dish. Cut
the chicken above into small pieces and remove the bones,
before putting into the curry sauce – make this a little thicker.

Curried Meat Balls

$1\frac{1}{2}$ lb. beef (or choose a mixture of beef and veal)
2 medium-sized onions
1 oz. butter
$\frac{1}{2}$ teaspoon ground ginger
1–2 teaspoons curry powder
2 oz. (1 cup) soft breadcrumbs
2 egg yolks
3–4 tablespoons thick cream
For frying and the sauce:
3 oz. ($\frac{3}{8}$ cup) cooking fat or butter

1 oz. ($\frac{1}{4}$ cup) flour
1–2 teaspoons curry powder
$\frac{1}{2}$ pint ($1\frac{1}{3}$ cups) white stock
$\frac{1}{4}$ pint ($\frac{2}{3}$ cup) thin cream or milk
seasoning
Garnish:
1–2 green peppers
3–4 tomatoes
cooked rice

Mince the meat very finely. Chop the onions very finely or grate coarsely. Heat the butter in a pan, stir in the onions and cook gently until nearly soft. Add the ginger and curry powder then the meat. Blend very thoroughly, then stir in the crumbs and egg yolks and mix well. Gradually add enough cream to give a soft creamy texture. Put into a cool place for about 30 minutes to stiffen slightly. Make into small balls the size of little walnuts. Heat the cooking fat or butter in a large frying pan. Put in the balls and brown, turning round several times. Lift the balls out of the pan on to a large plate.
Blend the flour with the fat remaining in the pan and cook for 1–2 minutes. Add the curry powder, then blend in the stock and bring to the boil. Cook gently until thickened, stir in the cream or milk and seasoning. Replace the meat balls and simmer gently for about 10 minutes.
Spoon the balls and sauce on to a very hot dish, garnish with rings of pepper, slices of tomato and the hot rice.
Serves 5–6.

Variation:
Creamed veal curry: Follow the recipe above, but fry small pieces of veal fillet in the butter instead of meat balls.

Ham and Chicken Mould

2 envelopes aspic jelly powder, enough to set 2 pints (5½ cups) liquid
2 pints (5½ cups) white stock or water
2–3 hard boiled eggs
about 1–1¼ lb. cooked chicken
about 1–1¼ lb. cooked ham (make a total of 2¼ lb. meat in all)
few cooked peas
large can asparagus tips

Dissolve the aspic in the stock or water according to the directions on the packet. Allow to cool. Pour a little into the bottom of a lightly oiled or rinsed 4-pint (10–11 cups) mould or basin and leave this to set. Shell the eggs, slice, then arrange in a neat design on the jelly. Spoon a very little aspic over the egg slices and put into the refrigerator or stand over a basin of ice. When the jelly is firm put a layer of neatly diced meat and peas into the mould, cover with liquid jelly. Leave once again to set.

Continue like this, using the very well drained asparagus for the final layer. Cover with the last of the jelly and leave until the mould is firmly set.

Dip the mould for a few seconds in warm water. Invert on to the serving dish and serve with salad.
Serves about 8.

Variations:
Ham and tongue mould: Use cooked tongue in place of the chicken.
Tomato-flavoured mould: Use tomato juice in place of stock or water. As this gives flavour to the mould ordinary gelatine may be substituted for aspic jelly.
Meat loaf: Mince the chicken and ham or ham and tongue, chop the eggs and the asparagus neatly. Make the jelly, allow it to cool and stiffen very slightly. Mix with the minced meats, eggs, asparagus and peas. Put into a mould or loaf tin and leave to set. Turn out and serve.

To complete the meal:
Any light dessert would be excellent or cheese and biscuits.

Creamed Kidneys

1 green pepper
1 red pepper
seasoning
8 lambs' kidneys
1 oz. ($\frac{1}{4}$ cup) flour

2 oz. ($\frac{1}{4}$ cup) butter
3 tablespoons ($\frac{1}{4}$ cup) dry sherry
$\frac{1}{4}$ pint ($\frac{2}{3}$ cup) thin cream
4–6 oz. ($\frac{1}{2}$–$\frac{3}{4}$ cup) long grain rice

Halve the peppers. Remove the cores and seeds then cut the flesh into neat strips. Blanch the strips of pepper by cooking them in boiling, well seasoned water for 3–4 minutes only, then drain well. Skin the kidneys, halve and remove the white cores. Season the flour, roll the kidneys in this.
Heat the butter in a large pan. Fry the strips of pepper for a few minutes. Lift out of the pan on to a dish and keep hot. Cook the kidneys in the remaining butter until tender. This takes 8–10 minutes. Turn the meat several times so it does not harden in cooking.
Blend the sherry and cream in a basin. Remove the pan from the heat, add the flavoured cream, stir well to mix the meat and sauce. Return to a low heat for 2–3 minutes only with some of the peppers.
Boil the rice in salted water while cooking the peppers and kidneys. Arrange in a ring in a hot dish. Spoon the kidneys and sauce in the centre and top with the remaining peppers.
Serves 3–4.
Variations:
Creamed liver: Diced veal or calves' liver could be used in place of the kidneys.
Creamed scampi: Use large prawns in place of the kidneys. Toss in the butter for 3–4 minutes only.
Creamed chicken: Use diced uncooked frying chicken instead of the kidneys. Turn in the butter for 8–10 minutes.
To complete the meal:
Serve with a tomato salad and follow with fresh fruit or stuffed peaches.
To serve for a buffet:
As the basic recipe.

Following spread: HAM AND CHICKEN MOULD

EGG DISHES

An egg provides the basis for light dishes more quickly than any other food and it is ideal if you do not want a heavy meal late at night. Do not imagine the basic ways of cooking eggs, i.e. boiling etc., provide only dull dishes. I hope the following suggestions disprove this.

Baked eggs:
The simplest way to bake an egg is to break it into a well buttered then heated oven-proof dish, top it with seasoning and butter and bake for just over 10 minutes in a hot oven, Serve with hot toast and butter.
To make the dish more interesting try the following:

Fish ramekins:
Blend the contents of a small can of tuna, salmon, crabmeat or about 6 oz. flaked cooked fish with seasoning and 3 tablespoons thick cream. Put at the bottom of 1 large or 4 smaller dishes. Break eggs on top (allow 1 or 2 per person) season well, then top with cream plus a little grated cheese (this can be omitted if wished). Bake for approximately 15 minutes in a hot oven.

Eggs à la Provencale:
Skin and slice 8 oz. tomatoes and fry in 1 tablespoon hot oil with a crushed clove of garlic (a small chopped onion can be added if wished). Season well and allow to simmer until a thick purée. Add a small amount of water if necessary. Meanwhile wash and slice 1 large or 2 small aubergines (egg plants) and fry in a little hot oil until tender. Put the aubergines into a well buttered, shallow oven-proof dish, season well and cover with thinly sliced tomatoes and 4–8 eggs. Top the eggs with a little melted butter and bake for 10–15 minutes in a hot oven until set. Spoon over the hot tomato purée and top with chopped parsley.

Preceding page: CREAMED KIDNEYS *(Photograph by National Dairy Council)*

To complete the meal:
Serve these dishes with salad and follow with cheese (unless this is part of the dish).

To serve for a buffet:
These dishes are only suitable if timed very carefully; over-cooking spoils any egg dish.

Boiled Eggs

Boiled eggs can not only be served in a cheese sauce, as in the recipe that follows, but can be coated with any type of savoury sauce, i.e. tomato, curry, anchovy, etc,. Here are some quick suggestions:

Curried eggs:
Make the quick curry sauce as page 77. Meanwhile boil 4 eggs (see page 48). Shell the eggs and put into the sauce.

Anchovy eggs au gratin:
Make a white sauce (as the recipe that follows) but omit the cheese and add the contents of half a small can of anchovy fillets (drain these well). Put 4 boiled eggs (see page 48) and the sauce into a dish, top with breadcrumbs and a little melted butter or margarine, crisp under the grill then top with the rest of the anchovy fillets and sliced tomatoes.

Eggs Au Gratin

4 eggs
1 oz. butter or margarine
1 oz. ($\frac{1}{4}$ cup) flour
$\frac{1}{2}$ pint ($1\frac{1}{3}$ cups) milk
seasoning

4 oz. (1 cup) grated Cheddar cheese
Topping:
2–3 tablespoons grated Cheddar cheese
2–3 tablespoons breadcrumbs

Boil the eggs, these can be firmly set or hard boiled, according to personal taste. Plunge into cold water to cool, crack the shells, then remove these.

Heat the butter or margarine in a pan, stir in the flour and cook for several minutes. Gradually blend in the milk and bring to the boil, then cook until the sauce has thickened. Season well, stir in the grated cheese. Do not continue cooking after the cheese has melted.

Arrange the whole or halved eggs in a dish, top with the cheese sauce then the grated cheese and crumbs and brown under the grill or in the oven.

Serves 2.

Corn Paella

3–4 rashers bacon
2 oz. ($\frac{1}{4}$ cup) butter
several cooked or canned potatoes
1 medium-sized can sweet corn

few olives or chopped parsley
4 eggs
2 oz. ($\frac{1}{2}$ cup) grated cheese
seasoning

Cut the bacon into strips, fry until nearly crisp. Add the butter, allow to melt, then add the diced potatoes, drained sweet corn and sliced olives or parsley. Beat the eggs, add the cheese and season lightly. Pour over the hot mixture in the pan and allow to set. Serve at once.

Serves 4.

Variations:

Speedy paella: Use about 4 oz. cooked rice (about 1 cup) instead of the corn. This is an ideal way of using up left-over rice.

Use cooked peas and carrots instead of the corn.

Use diced cooked or canned asparagus instead of the corn.

Omelettes

Allow 2 eggs per person for a small main dish omelette. Beat the eggs with seasoning, add any flavouring (see below) and add 1 tablespoon water to 2 eggs. Heat at least 1 oz. butter in a pan (never try and cook more than 3–4 eggs in a pan less than 6 inches in diameter, but do not use too large a pan so the mixture is too thinly spread). When the butter is hot, pour in the eggs and allow to set lightly at the bottom. Loosen the egg mixture from the sides of the pan with a knife, tilt the pan and let the liquid egg run to the sides of the pan. Continue like this until set to personal taste. Fold away from the handle, tip on to a hot dish.

Easy flavourings:
Add chopped mixed herbs; little grated cheese; fried mushrooms; chopped shell-fish; sliced fried peppers; diced cooked ham to the eggs.

Easy fillings:
Fill with grated cheese (this gives a more moist omelette than adding cheese to the eggs); fish, meat or poultry in a thick sauce; fried bacon and tomatoes; heated canned or cooked asparagus; diced cooked or canned new potatoes and diced cheddar cheese; cooked spinach by itself or in a cheese or white sauce; mixed cooked vegetables.

Tortilla:
This Spanish-type omelette is an ideal way of making a one-dish meal. Heat mixed cooked vegetables or just diced cooked potatoes, or any other combination of ingredients i.e. fish and vegetables, sliced salami and potatoes, shell-fish and onions, in hot butter or oil in the pan. Pour over the beaten eggs (see above) and cook the omelette. Serve as a flat omelette.

To complete the meal:
Serve the recipes given with toast, crispbread and butter.

50

Bornholm Omelette

7 oz. can herring fillets
few radishes
small piece lettuce
6–8 eggs
2 tablespoons thin cream or milk

seasoning
2 oz. ($\frac{1}{4}$ cup) butter
2 tablespoons chopped chives,
    spring onions or scallions

Cut the fillets into neat strips, slice the radishes and shred the lettuce, so the omelette is not kept waiting after cooking. Beat the eggs with the cream or milk and seasoning. Heat the butter in a large omelette pan, pour in the eggs and cook as page 50, until just set. Slide on to a hot dish (do not fold), top with the herring pieces, radish slices, shredded lettuce and chives, spring onions or scallions.
Serves 4–6.

To complete the meal:
Serve with crusty bread and have refreshing fresh fruit, such as oranges, afterwards.

To serve for a buffet:
This is not very suitable for a buffet unless using a table cooker or frying pan.

Soufflé Omelettes

Although traditionally filled with jam or other sweet ingredients a soufflé omelette can be served as a savoury dish. Take any omelette recipe, but separate the eggs. Beat the yolks with seasoning (or sugar for a dessert), add any other ingredients mentioned in the recipe. Fold in the stiffly whisked egg whites. Commence cooking the omelette in the usual way, but when half set take the pan to the grill and continue cooking under a medium heat. If the omelette pan is suitable it can be transferred to the oven.

Following page: BORNHOLM OMELETTE

Pastel De Tortillas (Omelette Cake)

8 eggs
seasoning
3 tablespoons water
about 2 oz. ($\frac{1}{4}$ cup) butter
Sauce:
$1\frac{1}{2}$ – 2 lb. tomatoes
2 oz. ($\frac{1}{4}$ cup) minced (ground) raw
  beef
1 clove garlic
1 onion
seasoning
good pinch dried or fresh basil

Layer one:
about 4 oz. (1 cup) mixed cooked
  vegetables
little butter
Layer two:
4 oz. (1 cup) mushrooms
1–2 oz. butter
Layer three:
4 oz. (about 1 cup) cooked
  shrimps or other shell fish
little butter

This is an unusual variation of the Spanish omelette or Tortilla. The omelettes are made as page 50 but do not cook these until all the fillings and sauce are ready.

To make the sauce, chop the tomatoes, put into a pan and simmer until the juice flows, then add the beef, crushed garlic, chopped onion, seasoning and herbs. Simmer for about 30 minutes, sieve if wished, then reheat. The sauce must be fairly stiff, so allow any surplus liquid to evaporate in an uncovered pan.

Heat the vegetables in the minimum of butter (they must not be greasy). Slice or chop the mushrooms, simmer in the butter. Toss the shrimps or shell-fish in butter.

Make four omelettes as page 50. Put the first omelette on a hot dish, cover with the vegetable layer, then add the second omelette and the mushroom layer, the third omelette and the shell-fish and the final omelette to cover. Top with some of the sauce and serve the rest separately.

Serves 4–5 as a main course, 8–10 as an hors d'oeuvre.

To complete the meal:
If serving as a main course follow with fruit; if serving as an hors d'oeuvre serve a cheese salad after this.

To serve for a buffet:
As this should be served immediately after cooking it would be unsuitable for a buffet.

Preceding page: PASTEL DE TORTILLAS

Eggs Ragoût-in a Pan

4 oz. streaky bacon, cut into thin
  slices
1 large onion
1–2 oz. cooking fat
few mushrooms (optional)

1 medium-sized can baked beans
seasoning
4–6 eggs
Garnish:
chopped parsley

Remove the rinds from the bacon, put these into a frying pan
and cook to extract all the fat. Dice the bacon and slice the
onion thinly and fry together for a few minutes, add a little
extra cooking fat if necessary, remove the rinds. Add the
sliced mushrooms if wished, and beans, heat thoroughly,
season well.
Make 4–6 'wells' in the mixture. Put a small knob of cooking
fat into each 'well', melt this, then drop in an egg and fry
for a few minutes.
Spoon on to hot serving plates and top with chopped parsley.
Serves 4–6.

Eggs in Corned Beef Hash

12 oz. can corned beef
about 8 oz. (1 cup) cooled mashed
  potatoes
seasoning
2–3 tablespoons milk

1–2 oz. cooking fat
4 eggs
Garnish:
2 tomatoes

Flake the corned beef and mix with the potatoes, seasoning
and enough milk to make a soft consistency. Heat a good knob
of cooking fat in a large frying pan. Form the mixture into
four rounds, put these into the frying pan and hollow out the
centre to make a nest shape. Fry steadily until golden
coloured. Add a little cooking fat to the centre of the corned
beef rounds, break an egg into these hollows and fry for a few
minutes. Lift out carefully and garnish with sliced raw tomato.
Serves 4.

PASTA DISHES

Pasta of various kinds is an excellent basis for a supper dish. Allow $1\frac{1}{2}$–2 oz. pasta per person (unless served with a very filling sauce as the recipe on page 58). Cook all pasta in plenty of fast boiling water – too little water means the pasta will stick – and never over-cook it, for this will make it lose both texture and flavour. Here are some quick ways to serve spaghetti (but other pasta could be used instead). The dishes are enough for 4 large or 6 smaller portions.

Spaghetti with eggs and anchovy fillets:
Cook 8 oz. spaghetti, drain then mix with the oil from 2 small cans anchovy fillets. Chop the fillets from one can and stir into the spaghetti with 2 tablespoons chopped spring onions or scallions and 4 sliced hard boiled eggs. Spoon into a hot dish or on to hot plates and top with the remainder of the anchovy fillets and with fried croûtons of bread and/or a few fried mushrooms.

Spaghetti with salami:
Cook 8 oz. spaghetti, drain. Meanwhile simmer 1 lb. chopped skinned tomatoes with $\frac{1}{4}$ pint ($\frac{2}{3}$ cup) water or stock; add 1 tablespoon oil, 1 tablespoon chopped parsley, 1 finely grated onion and 1 crushed clove garlic. Season well. Mix 4–8 oz. diced salami with the hot spaghetti, spoon on to hot plates or into a hot dish and top with the purée.

Spaghetti with Meat (Bolognese) Sauce:
Heat 2 tablespoons oil in a pan then add 1–2 finely chopped onions, 1 crushed clove garlic and 4 skinned chopped tomatoes. Stir in $\frac{1}{2}$ pint ($1\frac{1}{3}$ cups) stock or stock mixed with red wine and seasoning. Add 12 oz.–1 lb. raw minced steak, stir well and simmer steadily for about 1 hour. (Finely chopped herbs, grated or sliced carrots and green pepper may be added). Serve on cooked spaghetti and top with grated cheese.

LASAGNE AL FORNO *(Photograph by Eden Vale Limited)*

Lasagne Al Forno

Italian baked lasagne (with yogurt topping)

Meat sauce:
1 tablespoon oil
1 medium-sized onion
1 clove garlic (optional)
about 4–5 large tomatoes plus
$\frac{1}{4}$ pint ($\frac{2}{3}$ cup) brown stock or
use canned tomatoes with the
liquid from the can
1–2 teaspoons chopped mixed
fresh herbs
1 lb. lean minced beef
seasoning
Cheese sauce:
1 oz. butter
1 oz. ($\frac{1}{4}$ cup) flour

$\frac{1}{2}$ pint ($1\frac{1}{3}$ cups) milk
$\frac{1}{4}$–$\frac{1}{2}$ level teaspoon dry mustard
seasoning
about 3 oz. (up to 1 cup) grated
Gruyère or Cheddar cheese
Pasta:
4–5 oz. lasagne
at least 2 pints (5–6 cups) water
1 teaspoon salt
Yogurt topping:
5 oz. ($\frac{5}{8}$ cup) yogurt
1 egg
$\frac{1}{2}$ oz. flour
approximately 2 tablespoons
finely grated Parmesan cheese

First make the meat sauce, heat the oil and fry the chopped onion and crushed garlic for a few minutes. Add the skinned chopped tomatoes and stock or the canned tomatoes and liquid. Stir until a fairly smooth purée, then add the herbs and the meat. Cook gently, stirring from time to time to break up the lumps of minced beef. Season well. Allow to simmer gently for about 45 minutes.

Meanwhile make the cheese sauce, heat the butter, stir in the flour and cook for 2–3 minutes. Blend in the milk, bring to the boil and cook gently until thickened. Stir in the mustard, seasoning and cheese. Do not cook again after adding cheese. Put the lasagne into the boiling salted water, cook until tender, drain. Lasagne is often dried by draining it over the sides of a saucepan, so that you do not use damp pasta in the dish, and this gives a better result.

Cut the pasta into neat pieces, put in layers with the meat and cheese sauces, but end with lasagne. Top with the yogurt layer, made by blending the yogurt, egg and flour. Spread over the lasagne and sprinkle with the grated Parmesan cheese. Bake in the centre of a moderate oven, 375°F, Gas Mark 4–5,

for about 30 minutes. If you have allowed the pasta, meat and cheese sauces to cool, cook about 45 minutes at a slightly lower temperature. Serve at once.
Serves 4–5.

Variations:
The meat sauce may be thickened with a little cornflour if wished, although I prefer an unthickened sauce. To make a more interesting meat sauce, add a little red wine instead of stock or tomato liquid, a finely chopped green or red pepper and a few chopped mushrooms. You can also flavour the sauce with a little Worcestershire sauce.
A less elaborate dish is made by omitting the cheese sauce. Make the meat sauce, as the main recipe, but increase the amount of stock to $\frac{1}{2}$ pint ($1\frac{1}{3}$ cups), so the dish will be pleasantly moist. Cook and drain the lasagne. Put layers of the lasagne and meat sauce into the dish and cover each layer with a generous amount of grated Cheddar or grated Gruyère cheese or use the authentic Italian cheeses for this dish, i.e. a mixture of Mozzarella, Ricotta (cream cheese) and the strongly flavoured Parmesan. Put a good layer of grated cheese on top of the dish, but never use the cream cheese, as this burns very easily. Bake as the basic recipe.
Lasagne verdi: This is the name of the green lasagne (it is flavoured with spinach). It can be used in the basic recipe or any of the variations suggested, but it can be served with a good flavoured cheese sauce (see Macaroni Cheese and variations, page 62).

To complete the meal:
Serve with a green salad, tossed in well seasoned oil and vinegar or with a mixed salad. Sliced fennel is particularly good with pasta.

To serve for a buffet:
This is an ideal dish for a hot buffet for it is both easy to serve and to eat. It can be prepared beforehand and reheated, in which case make the sauce or sauces a little more liquid, since the pasta absorbs the liquid in standing.

Cannelloni Ripieni

Stuffing:
1 tablespoon oil
1 oz. butter
1 onion
4 oz. (1 cup) mushrooms
small portion green pepper
  (optional)
2–4 oz. (about $\frac{1}{4}$–$\frac{1}{2}$ cup) chopped
  ham
1 egg
2 oz. ($\frac{1}{4}$ cup) grated Parmesan
  cheese
seasoning

Sauce:
$1\frac{1}{2}$ oz. butter
$1\frac{1}{2}$ oz. ($\frac{3}{8}$ cup) flour
$\frac{3}{4}$ pint (2 cups) milk
seasoning
1 oz. ($\frac{1}{8}$ cup) grated Parmesan
  cheese
2 oz. ($\frac{1}{2}$ cup) grated Gruyère or
  Cheddar cheese

Pasta:
6–8 tubes cannelloni*
3–4 pints (8–11 cups) water
1 teaspoon salt

*Small pancakes can be used instead.

To make the stuffing, heat the oil and butter, add the finely chopped onion and chopped mushrooms. Cook gently until tender, then add the chopped green pepper and chopped ham and blend well. Stir in the egg, cheese and seasoning, do not cook again.

To make the sauce, heat the butter in the pan, stir in the flour and cook for several minutes, stirring well. Gradually blend in the milk. Bring to the boil and stir until thickened. Add the seasoning. Stir in the cheeses, but do not cook again.

Cook the cannelloni in the boiling salted water until tender. Drain, allow to cool, then put the filling into each 'tube' or pancake. If using pancakes roll firmly.

Spoon 2–3 tablespoons of the cheese sauce into an oven-proof dish, add the filled cannelloni, top with the remainder of the sauce. Heat for about 25 minutes, until the cheese sauce is delicately brown.

Serves 3–4.

To complete the meal:
Serve with broccoli, cauliflower or creamed spinach and follow with fresh fruit.

To turn into a buffet meal: See page 59.

Macaroni Cheese

3 oz. macaroni
salt
Sauce
$1\frac{1}{2}$ oz. butter or margarine
$1\frac{1}{2}$ oz. ($\frac{3}{8}$ cup) flour
$\frac{3}{4}$ pint (2 cups) milk
seasoning

4–6 oz. ($1-1\frac{1}{2}$ cups) grated cheese –
   use Cheddar, Gruyère, Dutch or
   other good cooking cheese
Topping:
2 oz. ($\frac{1}{2}$ cup) grated cheese (the
   variety as above)
2 tablespoons crisp breadcrumbs

Boil the macaroni in salted water until just tender, drain.
Make a white sauce with the butter or margarine, flour and
milk. Stir well until thickened and add seasoning and the
cheese. Do not cook again after adding the cheese. Stir in the
macaroni, tip into a hot dish, then top with the cheese and
breadcrumbs.
If the macaroni and sauce are both very hot, brown under a
hot grill; but if they have become cool it is better to heat
through for about 25 minutes in the centre of a moderate
oven, 350–375°F, Gas Mark 4–5.
Serves 4–6.

Variations:
Ham macaroni cheese: Mix diced cooked ham with the
macaroni and cheese sauce.
Macaroni florentine: Put a layer of cooked chopped or
sieved spinach at the bottom of the dish, then top with the
macaroni cheese mixture above and heat thoroughly.
Fish and macaroni pie: Cook and flake 8–12 oz. white fish.
Make the macaroni cheese recipe above, but use only 2 oz.
macaroni, so the mixture is less stiff. Add the flaked fish to
the cheese sauce, blend with the macaroni and heat as above.

To complete the meal:
Serve with salad and fruit.

To serve for a buffet:
Another excellent pasta dish for a buffet.

EASY RICE DISHES

Rice provides the basis for many economical and delicious dishes. Choose a long grain rice for this purpose, for the grains keep separate during cooking. If preferred buy brown rice (which retains more of the natural food value of rice) or use wild rice (actually this is not true rice, but is delicious, although somewhat costly).

To cook rice correctly:
There are several ways of boiling rice in salted water; the following two methods both ensure that the grains are not unpleasantly sticky.

Method 1: Weigh or measure the rice. To each 1 oz. of solid weight allow $2\frac{1}{2}$ fluid oz. of water (or stock or other liquid). To each cup of rice allow $2\frac{1}{2}$ cups of liquid. Put the rice with the cold liquid into a saucepan, add salt or seasonings and herbs to taste. Bring the liquid to the boil as quickly as possible, stir the rice with a fork. Cover the pan, lower the heat and simmer for approximately 15 minutes, by which time the liquid will have evaporated and the rice will be tender, but not sticky. This does not entail rinsing as Method 2.

Note: If using the partially cooked (or quick cooking rice as it is often called) allow only twice as much weight or double the measure of liquid since this will be tender more rapidly.

Method 2: To each 4 oz. ($\frac{2}{3}$ cup) rice allow 2 pints ($5\frac{1}{3}$ cups) water or stock. Bring the liquid to the boil, add seasoning and flavouring to taste. Put in the rice and cook rapidly until tender. Strain carefully, then pour boiling water through the rice to separate the grains (cold water could be used if you have plenty of time for reheating). Lay the rice out on a dish or large plate and heat gently in a very low oven.

Rice and cheese:
Cook the rice (either in water, stock or milk) season it well while cooking. Toss in plenty of grated cheese with butter and chopped herbs to give a moist texture and plenty of flavour.

Risottos

The Italian word Risotto means a savoury dish based upon rice
and the following recipes give a selection of ideas. All recipes
are based upon 6 oz. uncooked rice (i.e. 1 cup) and provide a
fairly substantial dish for 4 people or smaller portions for 6.

Fish risotto:
Heat 2 tablespoons oil in a strong saucepan, add a small
chopped onion and 1 crushed clove garlic (optional). Fry
gently for 2–3 minutes then add 6 oz. (1 cup) long grain
rice. Toss with the onion and garlic, then add 1 pint ($2\frac{2}{3}$ cups)
water or use fish or chicken stock, seasoning, and a good
pinch of lemon thyme together with the grated rind of 1
lemon and 2 teaspoons lemon juice. Bring to the boil, stir
briskly and simmer for 5 minutes (without covering the pan).
Dice 1 lb. firm white fish (discard any skin or bones) and put
into the rice mixture and continue cooking steadily until the
rice and fish are tender and the liquid absorbed sufficiently to
leave a pleasantly moist mixture. Top with chopped parsley,
and serve with grated cheese or top with anchovy fillets or
add shellfish to the mixture a short time before the end of the
cooking period. Stir gently once or twice during cooking.

Liver risotto:
Although chickens' livers are the most delicious in a Risotto,
any other tender liver could be used and this is an excellent
way of introducing it into the diet, particularly where it is
not over-popular (remember liver is not only a protein food,
but one of the main sources of iron in the diet). Heat 3
tablespoons oil in a strong saucepan, then fry 2 chopped
onions, 2–3 skinned chopped tomatoes and a few sliced
mushrooms (optional). Add 6 oz. (1 cup) long grain rice and
turn in the vegetable mixture. Add $1\frac{1}{4}$ pints (3 cups) water or
stock, seasoning and a pinch of sugar. Bring to the boil,
stirring well, simmer for 5 minutes, then add about 12 oz.
neatly diced lambs', calves' or chickens' livers, 2 oz. ($\frac{1}{3}$ cup)
sultanas and a little chopped parsley. Cook until tender. Top
with chopped parsley, rings of fried onions or mushrooms.

VEGETABLE RISOTTO

Vegetable Risotto

2 tablespoons oil
2 large onions
2 cloves garlic (optional)
1 lb. tomatoes
6 oz. (1 cup) long grain rice
1 pint (2½ cups) water or water
  with a little yeast extract
2–3 large carrots

few peas (fresh or frozen)
seasoning
few mushrooms
2–3 tablespoons chopped parsley
6–8 oz. (1½–2 cups) grated Gruyère
  or Cheddar cheese

Heat the oil in a strong saucepan, add the onions, cut into
neat rings, and the crushed cloves of garlic, if used. Fry for a
few minutes, then remove some of the onion rings.
Skin and slice the tomatoes, stir a few slices into the onion
mixture, together with the rice. Add the water or water and
yeast extract. Bring to the boil, then add the finely diced or
coarsely grated carrots and the peas. Cook steadily, seasoning
well, for about 10 minutes until the rice and vegetables are
beginning to become more tender. Add the remainder of the
tomato slices, the sliced mushrooms and the remaining onion
rings. Cook gently, stirring very little, until the rice is tender
and most of the liquid is absorbed. Blend in half the parsley
and half the cheese.
Pile on to a hot dish, top with the remainder of the parsley
and cheese.
Serves 4–6.

Variation:
Add pieces of diced cooked chicken or meat during cooking.

To complete the meal:
Serve with a well seasoned green salad.

To serve for a buffet:
Any risotto is ideal for a hot buffet dish. The risotto may be
partially cooked beforehand then completed at the last
minute. If you do this, increase the amount of liquid slightly,
so the mixture does not become too firm.

CHEESE DISHES

Although the pages that follow suggest a number of light dishes made with cheese, surely there can be no better light meal than a selection of interesting cheeses with salad and/or fruit. If you are not counting calories serve the cheese with crusty fresh bread, crispbread, biscuits and butter.

A cheese sauce can turn the humblest fare into a more interesting dish. Serve cheese sauce over eggs (see page 48), over cooked vegetables, with or over cooked fish of all kinds. A basic cheese sauce is made with 1 oz. butter or margarine, 1 oz. ($\frac{1}{4}$ cup) flour, $\frac{1}{2}$ pint ($1\frac{1}{3}$ cups) milk, seasoning and about 4 oz. cheese; the cup measure varies with the type of cheese – the lighter the cheese, e.g. Parmesan, the less full the cup. Choose a good cooking cheese to flavour the sauce, Gruyère, Emmenthal, Cheddar, Cheshire or Parmesan. Dutch cheese or processed cheeses are also good, although they give a milder flavour.

Children generally enjoy cheese, so sprinkle grated cheese or diced cheese over cooked vegetables, or use this as a sandwich filling.

Fried cheese:
Put thick slices of Cheddar or Gruyère cheese into the frying pan and cook for a few minutes; this is particularly good with fried slices of bacon or ham or with fried apple slices.

Baked cheese and eggs:
Put thin slices of Cheddar or Gruyère cheese into a well buttered shallow oven-proof dish. Break 1 or 2 eggs per person on top of the cheese, cover with a little thin cream and seasoning and a thick layer of grated or finely diced cheese. Bake for approximately 15 minutes just above the centre of a moderately hot oven, 375–400°F, Gas Mark 5–6. Serve with crispbread and salad.

Cheese Soufflé

1 oz. butter or margarine	seasoning
1 oz. ($\frac{1}{4}$ cup) flour	4 eggs
$\frac{1}{4}$ pint ($\frac{2}{3}$ cup) milk*	approximately 3 oz. ($\frac{3}{4}$ cup) grated cheese**

*This gives a fairly firm textured soufflé. If you are having this with vegetables, as a main course, I would increase the amount of liquid by up to an extra $\frac{1}{4}$ pint ($\frac{2}{3}$ cup). This means that you have a very soft texture in the centre which serves as a sauce with any vegetables.
**You can vary the cheese – Dutch Gouda gives a pleasant mild, creamy texture, a Cheddar or Gruyère a fairly definite taste and Parmesan a very strong taste and a drier texture.

Heat the butter or margarine in a large saucepan, stir in the flour then gradually blend in the milk. Cook until a thick sauce (if using the higher percentage of liquid it will be a coating consistency). Season well. Remove from the heat and add the egg yolks, then the cheese and finally fold in the stiffly beaten egg whites. Put into a greased soufflé dish. Bake in the centre of a moderate to moderately hot oven, 375–400°F, Gas Mark 5–6, for approximately 30 minutes. If using the larger quantity of liquid use the lower temperature so the mixture does not over-brown before it is cooked. Serve as quickly as possible.
Serves 4.

Variations:
Spinach soufflé: Ingredients as the basic recipe but substitute spinach purée for the milk. Cheese may be added if wished. Make and bake as above.
Fish soufflé: Ingredients as the basic recipe but use flaked cooked fish (white fish, salmon or shell-fish) in place of cheese and flavour the sauce with a few drops of anchovy essence. Make and bake as above.
Smoked haddock and cheese soufflé: This is a very pleasant combination. Follow the basic recipe but use only 2 oz. ($\frac{1}{4}$ cup) grated Parmesan cheese and 2–3 oz. cooked flaked smoked haddock. Substitute fish stock (or liquid from cooking the fish) for milk if possible.

CHEESE SOUFFLÉ *(Photograph by Dutch Dairy Bureau)*

Vegetable Soufflés

These make excellent light luncheon or supper meals. Cheese can be added for extra food value and flavour.

12 tablespoons (1 cup) soft purée of root vegetables, the most suitable are potatoes, carrots and swedes, or use a mixture of these
1 oz. butter or margarine

seasoning
herbs or spice to flavour (see method)
4 eggs
1–2 oz. ($\frac{1}{4}$–$\frac{1}{2}$ cup)* grated cheese (optional)

*Do not exceed this amount otherwise the mixture is too heavy. Parmesan cheese gives the strongest flavour.

Heat the purée with the butter or margarine, season well, add a little chopped chives or parsley or a mixture of fresh herbs. If preferred add a little ground nutmeg or cinnamon. Blend the egg yolks and cheese with the purée. Fold in the stiffly whisked egg whites. Continue as for the soufflé on page 68.

To complete the meal: Serve by itself and follow with fruit or a fruit salad.

Piroshki

Batter:
4 oz. (1 cup) flour, preferably plain
pinch salt
1 egg
$\frac{1}{2}$ pint ($1\frac{1}{3}$ cups) milk
oil for frying

Filling:
8 oz. (1 cup) cream or cottage cheese
1 oz. butter
1 egg
seasoning

Sieve the flour and salt, add the whole egg and milk to make a smooth thin batter. Use $\frac{2}{3}$ of the batter to make 6 medium-sized or 8 smaller pancakes. Blend the cheese, butter and egg yolk, season well. Whisk the egg white, fold into the remaining batter.

Put the filling into the pancakes, tuck in the ends to make very secure 'parcels'. Dip each 'parcel' into the remaining batter, fry in hot oil; although shallow oil could be used, a pan of deep oil is better.

Serves 4–6.

Variations:
Omit the seasoning, spread the pancakes with strawberry jam then with the cheese filling.

The method of coating the pancakes with batter is rather complicated so use all the batter for pancakes, fill, roll in the usual way. Put into a hot oven-proof dish, spread a little melted butter on top, sprinkle with grated cheese, heat for a short time.

To complete the meal:
It is better to serve the Piroshki by themselves. Follow by a refreshing sweet. If you choose the variation with jam and cheese, precede with a not-too-filling soup.

To serve for a buffet:
The pancakes could be made, filled, then just reheated or dipped in batter and fried at the last minute.

Pizza Pie

Base:
12 oz. (3 cups) plain flour
pinch salt
1 tablespoon olive oil
scant $\frac{1}{2}$ oz. fresh yeast*
scant $\frac{1}{4}$ pint (barely $\frac{2}{3}$ cup) water
Topping:
2 large onions
1–2 cloves garlic
1 tablespoon olive oil
$1\frac{1}{2}$ lb. tomatoes

1–2 tablespoons concentrated
  tomato purée
seasoning
$\frac{1}{4}$ teaspoon dried or 1 teaspoon
  fresh chopped oregano or
  marjoram
4–6 oz. ($1–1\frac{1}{2}$ cups) Cheddar,
  Mozzarella or Gruyère cheese
few anchovy fillets
few black olives
sprinkling grated Parmesan cheese

*Or $\frac{1}{4}$ oz. dried yeast.

Sieve the flour and salt into a mixing bowl. Make a well in the centre and add the oil. Cream the fresh yeast and add the tepid water, or sprinkle the dried yeast over the water. Pour the yeast liquid over the oil. Sprinkle flour over the yeast liquid. Cover the bowl with a cloth and leave in a warm place for about 15–20 minutes until the yeast liquid bubbles. Blend all the ingredients together and knead until smooth. Return to the bowl and cover. Leave in a warm place for about $1\frac{1}{2}$ hours until the dough has doubled its bulk. Knead again. Roll out to a 9–10-inch round then put on to a warmed, greased baking tray.

While the yeast dough is rising for the first time, prepare the topping. Peel and chop the onions and garlic. Toss in the hot oil, then add the skinned chopped tomatoes, the purée and seasoning. Simmer until the mixture is thick in an uncovered pan. Stir in the oregano or marjoram. Spread the tomato mixture over the yeast round. Top with the sliced or grated Cheddar, Mozzarella or Gruyère cheese, the anchovy fillets, olives and a sprinkling of Parmesan cheese. Allow to 'prove' for about 20 minutes (although this stage is not essential). Cook in the centre of a hot oven 425–450°F, Gas Mark 6–7 for about 15–20 minutes. If the yeast mixture is not quite cooked, put some foil over the topping to protect it, lower the heat to very moderate and leave a little longer. Serve hot or cold. **Serves 5–6.**

Variations:
Speedy Pizza: Ingredients as the basic recipe, but omit the yeast. Use self-raising flour or plain flour sieved with 3 teaspoons baking powder. Blend the oil and water (or you can use milk) with the sieved flour and salt. Knead lightly, roll into a round, add the topping and proceed as above.
Seafood Pizza: Ingredients as basic recipe plus about 4 oz. (1 cup) shelled prawns and use a whole can of anchovy fillets. Prepare as the basic recipe but add the prawns and most of the anchovy fillets to the cooked tomato mixture. Proceed as above.

Pizza Tart

Omit the ingredients for the base, as given in the recipe before. Instead of these make short crust pastry with 8 oz. (2 cups) flour, etc., (see page 28 under Old English Chicken Pie for the method of making the pastry). Roll out and line a 9–10-inch flan dish, flan ring (on an upturned baking tray) or shallow cake tin. Bake the pastry case 'blind' until pale golden brown – do not over-cook. Meanwhile prepare the ingredients as for the Pizza topping opposite. Put the warm mixture into the warm pastry. Add the cheese, anchovy fillets, etc., and heat in a moderately hot oven for about 7–10 minutes only.

To complete the meal:
Serve with salad.

To serve for a buffet:
An ideal hot or cold savoury dish for buffet parties. If you intend to cook the Pizza Pie beforehand, allow it to cool, then reheat for the party; leave the filling a little more moist. Brush with oil and sprinkle with a little extra cheese before reheating.
Do not put the filling into the tart too early as it could make this over-soft.

VEGETABLE DISHES

All too often the delicious flavour of vegetables is swamped by making them part of a main meal with meat and gravy, fish and sauce. When vegetables are at their best, serve them as a separate course.

Some of the most suitable vegetables to use in this way are:

Artichokes:
Boil in salted water and serve with plenty of well seasoned butter; dip the leaves into the butter and eat the fleshy base. Canned artichoke hearts can be heated and served with melted butter or with a cheese sauce (see page 67).

Asparagus:
Serve as artichokes above, or top with lightly set scrambled egg or melted butter and chopped hard boiled eggs together with a little grated cheese.

Cauliflower:
Serve topped with cheese sauce or in one of the ways suggested in the following pages. Cooked broccoli, either fresh or frozen, can be served in many of the same ways as cauliflower.

Courgettes:
One of the best dishes is to halve the unpeeled vegetables, and to simmer in a little salted water, until nearly tender. Put into an oven-proof dish and top with fried tomatoes and onions and heat in the oven. The halved cooked courgettes can also be topped with well seasoned scrambled egg and grated cheese.

Mushrooms:
Fry or bake mushrooms in a little butter, then fill with thick cheese sauce or scrambled egg blended with diced ham or crisply fried bacon.

Curried vegetables:

Many vegetables are excellent served in a curry sauce and this can be quickly prepared. Fry 1 chopped onion and 1 chopped dessert apple in $1\frac{1}{2}$ oz. margarine. Stir in 1 tablespoon cornflour, 1 tablespoon curry powder and $\frac{1}{2}$ pint ($1\frac{1}{3}$ cups) water or chicken stock. Add a few raisins, a little desiccated coconut, 2 tablespoons chutney plus seasoning and a squeeze of lemon juice. Either cook the vegetables in the sauce or add cooked vegetables to this and warm through.

The pulse vegetables

Peas, beans and lentils are ideal light dishes, for they are rich in protein and are therefore an excellent alternative to meat, fish, cheese or eggs.
They can be mixed with other vegetables to form a very pleasant meal.

Potato and Cheese Fritters

2 large potatoes
8 oz. (1 cup) cream cheese
2 oz. ($\frac{1}{2}$ cup) plain flour
1 egg

seasoning
little milk
oil for frying

Peel and grate the potatoes into a basin, add the cheese, flour, egg, seasoning and just enough milk to make the consistency of a thick batter. Heat a little oil in the frying pan and drop in spoonfuls of the mixture. Drain and serve.
Serves 4–6.

To complete the meal:

These are good with sliced tomatoes.

To serve for a buffet:

Fry the fritters, drain on absorbent paper, spread on flat dishes and reheat gently just before they are required.

Cauliflower Pancake Gâteau

Batter:
4 oz. (1 cup) plain flour
pinch salt
1 egg
½ pint (1⅓ cups) milk and water
oil or cooking fat for frying

Filling:
1 cauliflower
salt
little butter and thick cream
chopped chives and chopped
  parsley (optional)
To serve:
melted butter

Make the pancake batter by mixing all the ingredients together. Whisk or beat until smooth. Heat a little oil or cooking fat in a pan, pour enough of the mixture into the pan to give a thin coating. Cook until golden brown on the under side, turn and cook on the second side. Continue to make the rest of the pancakes. Keep hot.

Sprig the cauliflower and cook in boiling salted water for 10–15 minutes. Strain the cauliflower, tip into a hot basin and mash roughly with a fork. Blend with a little melted butter and cream. Spread each pancake with this mixture, pile one on top of the other. Top the pile with the chopped chives and parsley, if liked. Pour a little melted butter on top and serve at once. Serve with poached or baked eggs.
Serves 4–6.

Variations:
Cook creamed spinach can be used instead of cauliflower, or spinach and cauliflower can be used alternately.

Ways of serving pancakes:
Pancakes of all kinds make excellent light meals. The batter given in the recipe above is the standard recipe. The pancakes may be rolled round the filling rather than kept flat, as in the gâteau above.
If you wish to store pancakes to use on another occasion separate with squares of greaseproof or waxed paper. Wrap thoroughly and store in the refrigerator or freezer. 2–3 teaspoons oil added to the batter before cooking gives a better texture to the pancakes when they are to be frozen.

Pancakes Nicoise: Flavour thick tomato purée with chopped onions, garlic and chopped ham. Put into the pancakes.

Pancakes Florentine: Sieve cooked spinach, mix with a little thick cream and grated cheese or cheese sauce. Fill the pancakes.

Cauliflower Fritters

1 medium-sized cauliflower
salt
Batter:
4 oz. (1 cup) flour, plain or
  self-raising
pinch salt

2 eggs
$\frac{1}{4}$ pint ($\frac{2}{3}$ cup) water
4 tablespoons milk
oil or cooking fat for frying

Sprig the cauliflower and cook in boiling salted water for 10–15 minutes; take particular care that the vegetable is not over-cooked. Strain the cauliflower carefully, so the sprigs are not broken.

Seive the flour and salt, add the egg yolks, water and milk, then fold in the stiffly whisked egg whites. Heat the oil or cooking fat. While you can fry these fritters in shallow fat it is easier and better to use deep fat. Dip the sprigs into the batter and fry for 1–2 minutes only in the hot oil or cooking fat. Drain on absorbent paper.

To make a light supper dish, toss in grated Cheddar, Gruyère or Parmesan cheese.

Serves 4–8.

Variations:

Brussels sprouts or broccoli can be used instead of cauliflower.

Yogurt fritters: Use yogurt or soured cream instead of water and milk.

Tomato and cauliflower fritters: Use tomato juice instead of water and milk.

Corn and Cheese Fritters: Use the recipe above but use $\frac{1}{4}$ pint ($\frac{2}{3}$ cup) milk and 2 tablespoons water instead of the liquid above. Add 4 oz. ($\frac{2}{3}$ cup) grated Cheddar cheese and a small can drained sweet corn. Fry as above.

Cauliflower Basket

1 medium-sized cauliflower
salt
Cheese sauce:
1 oz. butter or margarine
1 oz. ($\frac{1}{4}$ cup) flour
$\frac{1}{4}$ pint ($\frac{2}{3}$ cup) milk
$\frac{1}{4}$ pint ($\frac{2}{3}$ cup) liquid from cooking
   the cauliflower

seasoning
4 oz. (1 cup) grated Cheddar cheese
2 eggs
1 tablespoon chopped gherkins
1 teaspoon capers
1 tablespoon chopped parsley
1 tablespoon chopped chives

Prepare the cauliflower, keeping it whole. Cook in boiling salted water until just tender, drain.

While the cauliflower is cooking, prepare the sauce. Heat the butter or margarine in a pan, stir in the flour and cook over a gentle heat for 2–3 minutes, stirring well. Gradually add the milk, bring to the boil, then add the cauliflower liquid and stir as the sauce thickens over a medium heat. Add seasoning and nearly all the cheese.

Hard boil the eggs, shell, chop and blend with the hot cheese sauce together with the gherkins, capers and herbs. Scoop out the centre part of the cauliflower. Put this on to a plate, chop coarsely and add to the sauce.

Stand the cauliflower in a hot serving dish. Pile the cheese mixture into the centre. Top with the remainder of the cheese and brown for 1–2 minutes under a very hot grill.
Serves 4–6.

Variation:
Omit the eggs and use shelled prawns or diced cooked ham instead.

To complete the meal:
The best accompaniment would be a tomato salad.

Aubergines Gratinées

4 small or 2 large aubergines
  (eggplants)
seasoning
2 tablespoons oil
8 oz. cooked ham
2 tablespoons chopped spring
  onions or scallions
2 oz. (1 cup) soft breadcrumbs

2 teaspoons chopped parsley
1 teaspoon chopped dill or other
  herbs
2 eggs
Topping:
crisp breadcrumbs
1½ oz. butter

Wash and halve the aubergines (eggplants) lengthways. Score
the skins with a sharp knife, sprinkle with salt and leave for
about 20 minutes. This lessens the slightly bitter taste, that
many people dislike. Heat the oil in a pan and fry the
aubergines (eggplants) on both sides until nearly cooked.
Lift out of the pan and arrange in a shallow oven-proof dish,
cut side uppermost.
Chop the ham very finely, mix with the spring onions or
scallions, breadcrumbs, herbs and eggs. Season well and
spread this over the top of the halved aubergines (eggplants).
Sprinkle crisp breadcrumbs over and moisten with melted
butter. Bake for 25 minutes in the centre of a moderate oven,
350–375°F, Gas Mark 4–5.
Serves 4.

Variations:
Top the aubergines (eggplants) with grated Parmesan cheese
instead of, or in addition to, the crisp breadcrumbs.
Use minced chicken or other meat in place of ham.
Fry tomatoes until a thick purée, seasoning well. Spread over
the halved partially cooked aubergines (eggplants), then put
on the topping as the basic recipe or one of the variations
and bake as in the basic recipe.

To serve for a buffet:
Although the recipe is excellent for a buffet the aubergines
(eggplants) are a little difficult to cut with a fork. Slice the

aubergines (eggplants), fry, then put into the dish, spoon the topping over and bake.

Beans Niçoise

1 lb. green beans
seasoning
Sauce:
1 lb. tomatoes
1 clove garlic

1 small onion
2 tablespoons oil
2 tablespoons chopped parsley

If using runner beans, slice in the usual way. French and haricot verts can be left whole, just remove the ends and string the sides if necessary. Cook in a little well seasoned water until nearly tender.
Meanwhile skin and chop the tomatoes, crush the garlic and chop the onion. Fry the onion and garlic in the hot oil in another saucepan, add the tomatoes and cook for a few minutes.
Strain the beans, save about $\frac{1}{4}$ pint ($\frac{2}{3}$ cup) of the liquid from the pan and tip this and the beans into the tomato mixture. Finish cooking, season to taste and top with the parsley.
Serves 4.

Variations:
Soaked cooked haricot (navy) or butter beans could be used instead, so could peas or soaked and cooked lentils. Do not use as much water with lentils, simply strain the lentils and tip into the tomato mixture with a few tablespoons of the liquid in which they have been cooked.

To complete the meal:
The vegetable course would be very satisfying, so follow with cheese and fruit.

To serve for a buffet:
Although this dish and the variations taste delicious they do not look particularly exciting for a buffet party.

French Fried Fennel

1 fennel root
2 oz. ($\frac{1}{2}$ cup) flour
1 egg
6 tablespoons ($\frac{1}{2}$ cup) milk

seasoning
oil or cooking fat for frying

Wash the fennel and slice the white root. Save the green leaves for garnish. Separate into rings. Mix the flour, egg and milk into a smooth batter. Season well. Dip the rings of fennel into the batter. Heat the oil or cooking fat (deep oil or cooking fat is better for frying this particular dish). Put in the coated rings and fry for 2–3 minutes only. This gives a cooked crisp outside without losing the natural firmness of the vegetable.
Serves 4.

SUSTAINING SALADS

The salads on this and the following pages are meant as a complete dish. Naturally you will want to make green salads (a mixture of all green salad ingredients plus cucumber, green pepper and celery) and mixed salads to serve with main dishes. All are suitable for buffets.

In order to make appetizing salads do prepare the lettuce or other salad greens well beforehand, i.e. wash, shake dry and allow time to crisp.

Choose a good variety of both colours and textures in your salad and when it is to be served as a main dish have a generous amount of protein food; if short of meat, fish or cheese then include beans or peas in the salad ingredients.

Herring Salad

8 rollmop herrings
4 large cooked potatoes or use
  8–12 small canned potatoes
2 tablespoons chopped spring
  onions or scallions
1 dessert apple

piece cucumber
good pinch curry powder
mayonnaise
cooked beetroot
lettuce
tomatoes
radishes

Divide the rollmop herrings into neat pieces, save about 1 tablespoon of the liquid from the jar (or use white vinegar). Dice the potatoes. Mix the herring pieces, potatoes and liquid from the jar or vinegar together, then add the spring onions or scallions, peeled and neatly diced apple, diced cucumber (remove peel if wished), the curry powder and enough mayonnaise to bind. Put into a basin and leave for a while if possible for the flavours to mix well.

Peel and dice the beetroot and stir gently into the mixture just before serving. If the beetroot is added too early it stains all the ingredients.

Arrange the lettuce on a dish, pile the salad in the centre and garnish with halved tomatoes and radishes.
Serves 4–6.

Variations:
Cooked herrings can be used in place of rollmop herrings, in which case use a generous 1 tablespoon vinegar to moisten the salad before adding the mayonnaise. This sharpens the flavour and makes sure it is not too insipid.
Use diced cooked white fish or white and shell-fish, but omit the vinegar in this case as it is too overpowering with white or shell-fish. Add a very little lemon juice and finely grated rind instead and omit the curry powder.
Mackerel makes an excellent alternative to herrings; as they are so much larger 3–4 will be sufficient.
The various flavoured canned herring fillets could be used in this salad.

Cheddar Salad Roll

1 lb. Cheddar cheese	up to $\frac{1}{4}$ pint ($\frac{2}{3}$ cup) mayonnaise
1 green pepper	or salad dressing
1 red pepper	few drops Tabasco sauce
2 hard boiled eggs	1 lemon
2 tablespoons chopped parsley	**Garnish:**
2 teaspoons capers	lettuce
	tomatoes
	cucumber

Grate the cheese fairly finely, then put into a mixing bowl. Dice the flesh of the peppers (discard cores and seeds). Shell and chop the hard boiled eggs. Add the peppers, eggs, parsley and capers to the cheese, then stir the mayonnaise or salad dressing in gradually; you need just sufficient to bind the mixture. If too soft it cannot be made into a roll. Mix in the Tabasco, the finely grated lemon rind and just a squeeze of lemon juice. Form into a roll and chill. Serve on a bed of lettuce with sliced tomatoes and cucumber.
Serves 4–6.

Sweet and Sour Chicken Salad

1 small cooked chicken
Marinade:
2 teaspoons French mustard
4 tablespoons white wine vinegar
6 tablespoons ($\frac{1}{2}$ cup) salad oil
2 cloves garlic
1 teaspoon soy sauce
1 tablespoon honey
seasoning

about 8 small pickled gherkins or
    2 larger pickled cucumbers
4 rings pineapple
1 tablespoon raisins
2 tablespoons blanched flaked
    almonds
Garnish:
endive or lettuce
sliced beetroot
sliced cooked potatoes

Cut the chicken into small neat pieces. Blend the mustard with
the white wine vinegar (if not obtainable use half white wine
and half white malt vinegar instead), then add the oil, crushed
garlic, soy sauce, honey and seasoning. Add the sliced
gherkins or pickled cucumbers and diced pineapple, raisins
and the pieces of chicken. Allow to stand for only 15 minutes.
If the chicken has not absorbed all the marinade then spoon
this out of the bowl and sprinkle over the salad at the last
minute. Stir the nuts into the mixture just before serving.
Arrange the endive or lettuce on a dish, pile the chicken
mixture in the centre and the sliced beetroot and potatoes
around the edge of the dish.
Serves 6.
Note: The vinegar will make the chicken over-soft, so do not
prepare too soon before serving.

Variations:
Use lean cooked pork or cooked ham instead of the chicken.
Omit the vinegar and oil and blend the chicken with
mayonnaise instead. Since this can be a little 'cloying' add a
good pinch curry powder and a little lemon juice to the
mayonnaise.

Hawaiian Salad

1 lettuce
1–2 heads chicory
about 8 oz. (1 cup) cottage cheese
fresh or canned pineapple rings
2–3 oranges

1 apple
piece cucumber
oil and vinegar dressing (see
  page 91)

Prepare the lettuce, put on a flat dish. Wash and separate the chicory leaves, arrange at either end of the dish. Spoon the cottage cheese into the centre of the lettuce, garnish with halved pineapple rings, orange segments and apple and cucumber slices (both dipped in oil and vinegar).
Serves 4.
Note: About 2 tablespoons mayonnaise can be blended into the cheese if wished.

Variations:
Use peach slices instead of pineapple.
Use cooked well drained prunes instead of the orange segments.
Top the cottage cheese with halved walnuts or other nuts.

Salad Marguerite

3–4 eggs
small cauliflower
8 oz. French or haricots verts
  beans
seasoning

8 oz. potatoes
small bunch asparagus or medium-
  sized can asparagus
mayonnaise
lettuce

Hard boil the eggs. Divide the cauliflower into neat sprigs and cut the ends from the beans. Halve these if fairly long. Cook the cauliflower and beans in salted water. The potatoes may be cooked in their jackets, or peeled or scraped and should be boiled steadily in salted water. Cook the asparagus in salted water or drain canned asparagus. Shell the eggs and allow to cool. Drain the cooked vegetables; skin the potatoes if these were cooked in the skins. Cut the potatoes and asparagus into neat pieces.

Mix the vegetables with mayonnaise and season generously. Allow to cool. Shred the lettuce, put into a bowl. Pile the mixed vegetables on top of this and coat with a little more mayonnaise. Cut the eggs into segments. Take out the yolks and chop these finely. Arrange the egg whites over the top of the salad to look like flower petals and place the yolks in the centre to resemble the stamens of the flowers.

Serves 4–6.

Variations:
Omit the beans and add diced tongue or cooked ham.
Use another mixture of vegetables in season, but if no meat is used the beans add to the protein content of this dish.
Blue cheese salad: Make the salad as above, but omit the eggs. Crumble about 6 oz. Danish Blue cheese, add to the mayonnaise and blend well, then use this to mix all the vegetables together.

Oil and Vinegar Dressing

3 tablespoons olive or good salad oil
up to 1 teaspoon French mustard
good shake salt
pinch sugar or little more if wished
shake pepper
$1\frac{1}{2}$ tablespoons lemon juice or vinegar

Blend the oil into the mustard, then add the other ingredients. If wished put into the liquidizer goblet and mix together.
It is worthwhile making a larger quantity and storing it in a screw-topped jar. Shake well before using.

Tongue and Chutney Salad

1 teaspoon curry powder
3 tablespoons chutney
1–2 tablespoons mustard pickles
4–5 tablespoons ($\frac{1}{3}$ cup)
  mayonnaise

12 oz. cooked tongue (cut in one
  thick slice)
2 hard boiled eggs
lettuce

Blend the curry powder, chopped chutney, finely chopped pickles and mayonnaise. Cut the tongue into narrow fingers, chop the eggs. Mix with the dressing, spoon on to a bed of lettuce.
Serves 4–5.

Ham in Horseradish Dressing

4–5 tablespoons ($\frac{1}{3}$ cup)
  mayonnaise
2–3 teaspoons made mustard
2–3 tablespoons grated
  horseradish or horseradish
  cream

12 oz. cooked ham (cut in one
  thick slice)
2 dessert apples
Garnish:
watercress

Blend the mayonnaise, mustard and horseradish. Cut the ham into strips, toss in the dressing and leave until ready to serve. Peel and dice the apples, but do not mix into the salad until just before serving. Put the salad into a shallow dish and garnish with watercress sprigs.
Serves 4–5.

Variations:
Pork salad: Lean cooked pork could be used instead of tongue or ham in either of these salads.
Chicken salad: Although all chicken could be used in either salad, the dressings blend better if half chicken and half tongue or half chicken and half ham are used in the recipes above.

92

SANDWICHES TO MAKE A MEAL

If the fillings or toppings are carefully chosen to include protein, then sandwiches are a good choice for a light meal. Choose reasonably fresh bread (and try less familiar types of bread), spread with butter, margarine or peanut butter, then add the filling and a second slice of buttered bread or put the toppings over the bread for open sandwiches.

Open sandwiches are not only more attractive in appearance but they enable far more filling to be used and much less bread; this is particularly important if watching your weight. These quick and easy ideas could be used for both the traditional closed sandwich and for open sandwiches.

Cheese:

Mix grated Cheddar cheese with chopped gherkins or mixed pickles. Put on crisp lettuce.

Mix cream cheese or grated cheese, blended with a little thick cream, with well drained, chopped canned pineapple.

Crumble Danish Blue cheese, mix with a very little mayonnaise and chopped nuts or finely chopped celery.

Eggs:

Mix lightly scrambled egg with chopped green pepper.

Blend chopped hard boiled eggs with mayonnaise and prawns.

Mix chopped hard boiled eggs with a little mayonnaise, curry powder and chopped watercress.

Blend mashed sardines, a little lemon juice and chopped hard boiled eggs.

Fish:

Blend flaked cooked kippers with butter to bind, finely chopped spring onions or scallions and cucumber.

Cream cooked cod's roe with a little mayonnaise, a few drops anchovy essence and a little skinned chopped fresh tomato. Season well.

More Sandwich Fillings or Toppings

Meat:
Mix crisply fried bacon and liver pâté.
Mix chopped ham with Russian salad (cooked vegetables in
a thick mayonnaise).
Chop crisp bacon finely and blend with cream cheese. Top
with sliced tomatoes and sliced cucumber.
Cut chicken and ham into neat matchsticks. Blend with
cottage cheese and top with strips of cooked and very well
drained prunes.
Slice cooked pork and top with apple jelly and watercress.
Slice cooked beef and top with red cabbage.
Slice cooked lamb and top with mayonnaise, flavoured with
a very little chopped mint and blended with finely chopped
spring onions or scallions.

Toasted Sandwiches

Toast then butter bread (try a variety of breads) and
sandwich two slices with hot or cold fillings. If the filling is
to be hot prepare this before toasting the bread.

Cold fillings:
Mix sliced raw mushrooms with cream cheese and lettuce.
Blend chopped shell-fish or flaked salmon or tuna with diced
cucumber and mayonnaise; also try flavouring shell-fish with
curry.
Mash sardines, canned herrings or canned pilchards with
lemon juice, finely chopped gherkins and pickled onions.

Hot fillings:
Scrambled eggs blended with minced or chopped chicken,
ham, tongue or fish.
Fried eggs and crisply fried or grilled bacon, or fried eggs and
sliced fried mushrooms, sliced fried sausages or fried
tomatoes.

Cooked bacon and fried banana, pineapple or apple rings, or hot cooked prunes.

Boiled salted beef, lettuce and horseradish cream.

It spoils cheese to heat it twice, so put any cheese topping on one slice of buttered toast, heat for a few minutes until the cheese melts then top with the second slice of toasted buttered bread. Choose a good cooking cheese – Cheddar, Gruyère, Emmenthal, Dutch Edam or Gouda.

Top sliced cheese with anchovy fillets.

Top sardines with thinly sliced cheese.

Top slices of lean ham with mustard pickles then a thick layer of grated or sliced cheese.

Top cooked tomatoes with sliced cheese.

To complete the meal:
Have a generous-sized mixed salad and fruit.

To serve for a buffet:
Have an informal 'help yourself' sandwich buffet. Make the table look gay with open sandwiches. Have a toaster on the table with bowls of filling so everyone may make their own toasted sandwich.

Fried Sandwiches

8 slices of bread	1 egg
butter or margarine	4 tablespoons milk
filling (see method)	cooking fat for frying

Spread the bread with butter or margarine. Put the filling over half the slices of bread and top with the remainder. Beat the egg and milk, then dip the sandwiches in this mixture very briefly. Fry in a little hot cooking fat until crisp and brown on either side and serve at once.

Fillings: Slices of cheese topped with cooked ham.
Flaked salmon and tuna, flavoured with grated lemon rind and juice and topped with sliced hard boiled egg.
Rashers (slices) of lightly cooked bacon topped with pâté.

LIGHT DESSERTS

Fresh fruit is one of the best light desserts to serve for supper and this can be made more interesting in the following ways:

Apples:
Slice, core, dip in lemon or orange juice and top with dried fruit soaked in sherry or lemon or orange juice.

Bananas:
Mix with a custard sauce or mash and blend with ice cream and top with grated chocolate.
Coat the skinned bananas with sieved apricot jam and roll in chopped nuts.

Grapefruit:
Mix the segments of fruit with other fresh fruit. Put back into the fruit skins, top with sugar and a little sherry. Either serve cold or heat for a few minutes under the grill.
Blend the grapefruit segments with lightly whipped cream and soft fruit (raspberries or strawberries etc.) and a little sugar.

Pears:
Coat peeled, cored dessert pears with hot chocolate sauce.
To make this, melt 4 oz. plain chocolate in a basin over hot water, adding about 2 teaspoons water and a small knob of butter. This is sufficient to coat 2 large pears. Serve with cream or ice cream.

Peaches:
Skin (by dipping for a few seconds only in boiling water).
Halve if wished, then bake in the oven with brown sugar and rum or brandy.
Slice the skinned peaches and sprinkle with kirsch or white wine and chopped nuts.

Pineapple:
Peel and cut into slices. Remove the core, sprinkle with kirsch or dice the pineapple and mix with soft cream or cottage cheese. This will appeal to people who do not like a very sweet dish.

Beignets Aux Cerises (French Cherry Fritters)

Sauce:
1 lb. black or Morello cherries
$\frac{1}{4}$ pint ($\frac{2}{3}$ cup) water
2–4 oz. ($\frac{1}{4}$–$\frac{1}{2}$ cup) sugar
1 teaspoon arrowroot
3–4 tablespoons ($\frac{1}{4}$ cup) cherry
  brandy

Choux pastry:
$\frac{1}{4}$ pint ($\frac{2}{3}$ cup) water
1 oz. butter
3 oz. ($\frac{3}{4}$ cup) flour, plain or
  self-raising
pinch sugar
2 eggs
1 egg yolk
oil for frying

Put the cherries, water and sugar into a pan and simmer for about 5 minutes. Blend the arrowroot with the cherry brandy, stir into the cherry mixture, boil steadily, stirring well, until thickened. Keep hot.

Heat the water and the butter in a saucepan. When the butter has melted add the flour, sieved with sugar. Stir the mixture over a low heat until if forms a firm ball. Remove the pan from the heat and gradually add the beaten eggs and egg yolk.

Heat the oil to about 365°F, i.e. until a cube of day-old bread turns golden brown in about 30 seconds. Either put spoonfuls of the mixture into the hot oil, or put the choux pastry into a cloth bag with a 1-inch plain pipe. Squeeze the choux pastry through the pipe with one hand and cut off $1-1\frac{1}{2}$-inch lengths with kitchen scissors. Fry steadily for about 6–8 minutes until golden brown, lift out of the oil, drain on absorbent paper. Keep hot on a flat dish in a low oven.

Pile fritters into a pyramid and serve with the hot sauce.
Serves 6–8.

To complete the meal:
As this dessert is rich and satisfying and also demands a considerable amount of attention when cooking, precede with a salad.

To serve for a buffet:
Only suitable if you have quite an elaborate table cooker.

Meringues

2 egg whites

4 oz. ($\frac{1}{2}$ cup) castor sugar or use half castor and half sieved icing sugar

First check that the bowl is free from grease and that the egg whites are not too cold. If you have brought them out of the refrigerator allow to stand for an hour before whisking. Separate the egg yolks from the whites, cover the yolks with a little cold water to prevent them hardening; store in a cool place until they may be used.

Check no yolk has gone into the whites. If there is a particle remove with the half egg shell as a scoop or the corner of a damp, clean tea towel or damp kitchen paper. Whisk the egg whites until very stiff. If they seem slow in whisking, after taking the precautions above, then it may be the kitchen is too hot, so move to an open window. The egg whites are sufficiently stiff when they stand up in peaks and you can turn the bowl upside down without the mixture moving. There are several ways of incorporating the sugar. The best way is gradually to beat in half the sugar, then fold in the remainder gently and slowly. A softer meringue is given if you gradually fold in all the sugar and a very firm meringue (only successful if you have a mixer) is obtained if you gradually beat in all the sugar.

Brush the baking trays with a very little oil or butter, or brush greaseproof paper on the trays with oil. Either spoon or pipe the meringues on to the trays. Bake in the coolest part of a very slow oven, 225–250°F, Gas Mark 0–$\frac{1}{2}$, for about 2 hours until crisp, but still white. Lift from the tin with a warm, but dry, palette knife. Store in an airtight tin until ready to fill with whipped cream or ice cream.

Variations:

Add 1 level teaspoon sieved cocoa or $\frac{1}{2}$ teaspoon instant coffee powder to each 2 oz. ($\frac{1}{4}$ cup) sugar.

To complete the meal:

Meringues are very sweet, so serve after a refreshing salad.

Caramel Custard

Caramel:
3 tablespoons granulated or
   castor sugar (or equivalent in
   loaf sugar)
5 tablespoons ($\frac{1}{2}$ cup) water

Custard:
4 eggs
1 tablespoon sugar
1 pint ($2\frac{2}{3}$ cups) milk

To make the caramel, put the sugar and 3 tablespoons ($\frac{1}{4}$ cup)
of the water into a strong saucepan. Stir over a low heat until
the sugar has dissolved. If the sugar and water splash against
the sides of the saucepan brush with a pastry brush dipped in
cold water. This helps to prevent the mixture crystallizing.
Allow the sugar and water syrup to boil steadily until golden
brown, add the extra water and heat. Coat a 7–8-inch, oval or
round oven-proof dish with the caramel, cool. Blend the eggs,
sugar and warmed milk into the dish, stand in a container of
cold water, bake in the centre of a slow oven, 275–300°F,
Gas Mark 1–2, for $1\frac{1}{2}$–2 hours until firm. Cool for 10 minutes,
invert on to a serving dish.
Serves 4–6.

Variations:
Omit the caramel sauce and just bake the custard mixture. If
baking in a shallow pie dish you will find the cooking time
will be about $1\frac{1}{4}$ hours.
4 eggs make a very firm custard, you may only require to use
2 eggs.
The custard can be flavoured with a little chocolate powder,
cocoa, coffee essence or instant coffee.

To complete the meal:
These light custard desserts are ideal after a fairly substantial
main course.

To serve for a buffet:
Caramel custard is an ideal buffet party dessert for it is easy
to serve and eat.

Fruit Flans

The flan may be filled with cooked, canned, frozen or raw fruit. If using cooked or canned fruit strain carefully. If using frozen fruit allow to defrost lightly and strain. If using raw fruit make a syrup of $\frac{1}{2}$ pint ($1\frac{1}{3}$ cups) water boiled with approximately 4 oz. ($\frac{1}{2}$ cup) sugar (more or less as required) and simply put the raw strawberries, cherries or other fruit in the warm syrup for 2–3 minutes then strain. In this way the fruit absorbs the flavour of the syrup but does not become over-softened.

Make the fleur pastry as the recipe below, or use short crust pastry (see page 25) made with 6 oz. ($1\frac{1}{2}$ cups) flour etc. Roll out and line the flan case, or flan ring on an upturned baking tray or shallow baking tin. Fill with greaseproof paper and beans or crusts of bread to keep the pastry a good shape. Bake in the centre of the oven until golden brown (approximately 20–25 minutes); use a moderately hot oven, 400°F, Gas Mark 6 for fleur pastry and a hot oven, 425°F, Gas Mark 7 for short crust. Allow the pastry to cool, arrange the cold fruit in this. Measure the syrup and to each $\frac{1}{4}$ pint ($\frac{2}{3}$ cup) allow 1 teaspoon arrowroot or cornflour. Blend with the liquid and boil until thickened and clear. Cool slightly then brush over the fruit. Alternatively a biscuit crumb crust may be used. For this cream 4 oz. ($\frac{1}{2}$ cup) butter and 2 oz. ($\frac{1}{4}$ cup) castor sugar. Add 8 oz. crusted biscuits. Form into a flan case and chill.

Fleur Pastry

3 oz. ($\frac{3}{8}$ cup) butter or best quality margarine
2 oz. ($\frac{1}{4}$ cup) castor sugar

1 egg yolk
6 oz. ($1\frac{1}{2}$ cups) flour, preferably plain
little cold water

Cream the butter or margarine and sugar until soft and light. Beat in the egg yolk, add the sieved flour, blend with a palette knife. Gradually stir in enough water to bind.
To complete the meal:
Serve after a light main course.

Jellied Fruit Snow

½ pint (1⅓ cups) thick sweetened
   fruit purée*
1 teaspoon powdered gelatine
2 tablespoons water or fruit juice

¼ pint (⅔ cup) thick cream
3 egg whites
To decorate:
lemon slices (optional)

*In the picture apple purée was used and tinted with a little green colouring.

Warm the purée gently. Soften the gelatine in the cold water or fruit juice. Mix with the warm purée and stir until dissolved. Allow to cool, the fold in half the lightly whipped cream and 2 stiffly beaten egg whites. Spoon into 4–6 serving glasses and allow to set lightly (this will never be sufficiently stiff to turn out). Whip the remainder of the cream and the third egg white in separate basins, fold together and pile on top of the dessert. Decorate with lemon slices if wished.
Serves 4–6.

To use Gelatine

The instructions on the packet will give exact quantities. Generally one uses 1 envelope, which is ½ oz. or 1 tablespoon to 1 pint (2⅔ cups) clear liquid or half this quantity for thickened liquids, or the equivalent in sheet gelatine. Put the gelatine into a basin, add 2–3 tablespoons (¼ cup) cold liquid from the 1 pint (2⅔ cups). Stand the basin in, or over, a pan of hot water, leave until the gelatine has dissolved. There is no need to stir as the gelatine softens, do this just before blending with the other ingredients. Heat the remainder of the liquid, pour over the gelatine, stir until well blended. Rinse a mould or basin with cold water, leave damp. Pour in the jelly, when set invert on to a damp serving dish. This means you can slide the jelly easily into the centre of the dish.

Fruit Fool

Fruit fools, or to give the dessert its correct name, fruit foules, are a delicious mixture of smooth fruit purée and custard or cream.

1 pint (2⅔ cups) thick sweetened fruit purée*

1 pint (2⅔ cups) thick sweetened custard**

*Made by cooking fruit with the minimum of liquid then sieving or emulsifying or simply by sieving or emulsifying fresh fruit.
**Made with custard powder or eggs.

Blend the cold fruit with the cold custard and spoon into glasses or individual dishes. Chill and serve as cold as possible. The fools may be decorated with desiccated or grated coconut, cherries, etc.
Serves 4–6.

Variations:
With all cream: Whip 1 pint (2⅔ cups) thick cream, sweeten and fold into the fruit purée. As this is rather a rich dessert you can serve fairly small portions with sponge cake or plain sweet biscuits. Use half cream and half custard if preferred.
Home-made fruit ice cream: The version of fruit fool with all cream may be frozen to make a delicious ice cream.
Fruit Mousse: Use only ½ pint (1⅓ cups) custard or whipped cream to the fruit purée. Whisk 2 egg whites very stiffly, fold in 1 oz. sugar, then fold this into the mixture. Spoon into glasses and chill.

To complete the meal:
This type of dessert is ideal for a light supper or luncheon dish, for it is easy to digest and refreshing.

To serve for a buffet:
Decorate the fruit fool mixture in an interesting way for a party dessert. Keep in the refrigerator as long as possible so it really is very cold.

Lemon Sorbet

lemons
water
sugar

gelatine
egg whites

If lemons are plentiful and inexpensive there is no need to make use of the skin (which can provide plenty of flavour). Simply extract the juice from the lemons and dilute with water to give a good strong flavour (all lemon juice without any water tends to be a little sour for some people).

If you are economizing on lemons then pare the top rind from the fruit (do this thinly, so you take only the top 'zest' and none of the rather bitter white pith). Put the rind into a saucepan with a little water, simmer for 5–10 minutes, strain and add to the lemon juice.

To each 1 pint (2⅔ cups) liquid allow about 2 oz. (¼ cup) sugar. Warm the liquid slightly so the sugar dissolves well. If you intend eating the sorbet within 24 hours after making it is not essential to use gelatine, but this serves a very useful purpose in that it helps to prevent crystals of ice forming in the sorbet.

Allow 1–2 teaspoons gelatine (use the greater quantity if keeping the sorbet for some time) to each pint (2⅔ cups) liquid. Soften the gelatine in cold liquid then dissolve (see page 104) in the warm lemon liquid. Pour the mixture into a freezing tray and freeze lightly.

To each 1 pint (2⅔ cups) lemon liquid allow 2–3 egg whites and 1 oz. sugar. Whisk the egg whites until very stiff, gradually whisk in the sugar, then blend this meringue with the half frozen lemon mixture, do this gently and carefully, so you do not lose the light texture or make the lemon mixture too liquid. Return to the freezing tray and freeze lightly.

Note: There is never any need to alter the cold control on either a refrigerator or freezer, sorbets can be frozen at normal settings.

Variation:
Use other fruit juice or fruit purées in place of the lemon.

JELLIED FRUIT SNOW *(Photograph by Fruit Producers' Council)*

Orange Sponge

3 large eggs
3–4 oz. ($\frac{3}{8}$–$\frac{1}{2}$ cup) castor
  sugar
finely grated rind of 1–2 oranges
3 oz. ($\frac{3}{4}$ cup) flour*
1 tablespoon hot orange juice

Filling and decoration:
orange marmalade or orange curd
$\frac{1}{2}$ pint ($1\frac{1}{3}$ cups) thick cream
little sugar
Curaçao (optional)
crystallized orange slices

*So much air has been beaten into the eggs and sugar that a raising agent is really unnecessary, but you can use self-raising flour if wished.

Put the eggs and sugar (the larger quantity produces a lighter sponge) into a basin and whisk hard until a thick mixture. You should see the mark of the whisk. Add the orange rind. Sieve the flour very well, then fold into the whisked eggs with a metal spoon or palette knife; add the hot orange juice. Divide between two 7–8-inch well greased and floured sandwich tins or tins lined with greased greaseproof paper. If preferred coat the tins with fat then with an equal amount of castor sugar and flour.
Bake above the centre of a moderately hot oven, 400°F, Gas Mark 5–6, for approximately 15 minutes. If preferred, bake in one prepared cake tin for 30–35 minutes in the centre of a very moderate to moderate oven, 325–350°F, Gas Mark 3–4. Cool for 2–3 minutes before turning out of the tin or tins. When cold, sandwich the sponges together with marmalade or orange curd and a little whipped cream, or split the one cake if wished and fill. Sweeten the remainder of the cream and flavour with a few drops of Curaçao if liked. Pipe round the edge of the sponge. Decorate with the orange slices.

Variation:
Lemon sponge: As the Orange Sponge, but use lemon rind and juice, fill with lemon curd and cream and decorate with fresh lemon slices. If wishing to flavour the cream use an apricot brandy.

Grape Meringue Flan

10–12 bought small meringues or home-made (see page 100)
2 oz. ($\frac{1}{4}$ cup) butter
3 oz. (nearly $\frac{1}{2}$ cup) soft brown sugar
3 oz. (nearly $\frac{1}{2}$ cup) demerara sugar
8 level tablespoons ($\frac{1}{2}$ cup)* golden syrup or light corn syrup

8 oz. bran buds or other breakfast cereal
Filling:
8 oz. white grapes
2–4 oz. black grapes
4 level tablespoons sieved apricot jam
3 tablespoons ($\frac{1}{4}$ cup) water

*Generous measure.

If making meringues prepare these first (see page 100).
Melt the butter, the sugars and syrup in a large pan. Remove from the heat, add the bran buds or other cereal. Mix well then press into an 8-inch flan ring on a serving plate. Leave in a cool place for 2–3 hours to harden.
Halve the grapes, remove the pips. Heat the jam and water until a smooth glaze. Arrange the grapes in the flan and brush with the warm glaze. Leave to cool then put the meringues round the edge. Serve with cream.
Serves 5–6.

Variations:
Use crushed biscuit crumbs instead of bran buds.
Top with other fresh fruit; as this is a very sweet base do not use sweetened canned fruit.
Note: Do not put the meringues round the flan until ready to serve as the jam could soften them.

To complete the meal:
This is a very satisfying dessert and could be preceded with a salad or egg dish.

To serve for a buffet:
An ideal dessert – it looks attractive and can be prepared beforehand, but see Note above.

Orange Cheese Cake

Coating:
6 oz. digestive biscuits
2 oz. ($\frac{1}{4}$ cup) butter
1 tablespoon honey
grated rind 2 oranges
2 oz. ($\frac{1}{4}$ cup) castor sugar
Filling:
2 oz. ($\frac{1}{4}$ cup) butter
grated rind 1 orange

3 oz. ($\frac{3}{8}$ cup) castor sugar
2 eggs, separated
1 oz. ($\frac{1}{4}$ cup) cornflour
12 oz. ($1\frac{1}{2}$ cups) cottage cheese
2 tablespoons orange juice
To decorate:
little sieved icing sugar
canned mandarin oranges

Crush the biscuit crumbs until most of them are very fine, but keep some crumbs a little coarser (see the picture). Cream the butter, honey, orange rind and sugar. Add the crumbs and use to line the sides and bottom of a 7–8-inch cake tin – choose a tin with a loose base.
Cream the butter, orange rind and castor sugar together. Add the egg yolks, cornflour, cottage cheese (this can be sieved if wished, but it is not essential) and orange juice. Lastly, fold in the stiffly whisked egg whites. Spoon into the biscuit case and bake for approximately $1\frac{1}{4}$ hours in the centre of a slow to very moderate oven, 300–325°F, Gas Mark 2–3, until firm but pale golden. Allow to cool in the oven with the heat turned off (this stops the cake sinking).
Remove from the cake tin. Sprinkle icing sugar over the top of the cheese cake and decorate with well drained mandarin orange segments.
Serves 7–8.

To complete the meal:
A cheese cake is very sustaining so a light salad would be an ideal main course. The Orange Sponge on page 108 would be ideal after a filling soup.

Mainly for Buffets

Throughout this book you will find suggestions for adapting the light dishes for a buffet meal. In the pages that follow all the dishes are chosen specifically for a buffet, as they are not sufficiently sustaining for a main dish.

To make a perfect buffet table I would suggest either fish cocktails (as on page 113) or soup when the weather is cold. Arrange dishes of croûtons beside the soup.

Fried croûtons:

Dice bread and fry until crisp and golden brown. Drain on absorbent paper. These can be made beforehand and warmed on flat dishes just before the party. Toasted croûtons tend to become soft with standing.

Garlic croûtons:

Prepare as above, then toss in garlic salt. Another alternative would be to have diced melon or grapefruit cocktails (see page 126).

The choice of main dishes is almost endless (see the fish, meat and cheese dishes in this book) and have several bowls of gay looking salads to serve with these and a dish of home-made mayonnaise (see page 116).

Choose a variety of desserts and an attractive cheese board for a simple, but elegant buffet table.

Fish Cocktail

Although most fish can be used in a cocktail it is usual to
select shell-fish. A mixture of different shell-fish (cooked
mussels, crab and prawns) makes a more interesting cocktail
than if one variety only is used. Pay attention to the
flavouring of the sauce, for this is very important; shred the
lettuce finely, since the cocktail is eaten with a small spoon
and fork and large pieces of lettuce can be difficult to manage.

Sauce:
5–6 tablespoons ($\frac{1}{3}$–$\frac{1}{2}$ cup)
  mayonnaise
1 tablespoon thick cream
$\frac{1}{2}$ tablespoon lemon juice
1 tablespoon fresh or canned
  tomato purée or use tomato
  ketchup if you like a slightly
  sweet flavour
1 tablespoon dry sherry (optional)

few drops Worcestershire and/or
  Tabasco sauce and/or soy sauce
approximately 6 oz. ($\frac{3}{4}$ cup) shelled
  prawns or other shell-fish or a
  mixture of fish
$\frac{1}{2}$ small lettuce
Garnish:
1 lemon
parsley
paprika

Blend all the ingredients together for the sauce; this should
pour easily, so if it is too thick add a little more cream. Blend
most of the sauce with the fish, but save a little for the
topping. Shred the lettuce finely, put into 4–5 glasses, top
with the fish and sauce. Spoon the remaining sauce on top.
Top with wedges of lemon, sprigs of parsley and paprika.
Serve as cold as possible. It is ideal if the cocktail can be
served on crushed ice.
Serves 4–5.

Lemon Mayonnaise:
Flavour home-made (see page 116) or commercial mayonnaise
with very finely grated lemon rind and lemon juice.

Anchovy Boats

Pastry:
6 oz. (1½ cups) plain
  flour
seasoning
pinch dry mustard
3 oz. (⅜ cup) butter
2 tablespoons grated
  Parmesan cheese
1 egg yolk
little water to mix
Filling:
can anchovy fillets
3 eggs
2 tablespoons thick cream
pepper

Sieve the flour, seasoning and mustard. Rub in the butter,
add the cheese, egg yolk and water to mix. Roll out thinly,
line 12 boat-shaped tins. Chop the anchovy fillets, put into
the pastry cases. Beat the eggs and cream, add a shake of
pepper. Spoon the egg mixture over the anchovies. Bake
towards the top of a moderately hot to hot oven, 400–425°F,
Gas Mark 6–7 for 12–15 minutes. Serve hot.
Makes 12 boats.

Variations:
Caviare boats: Make the boats as above. Prick well, bake
'blind' until crisp and golden brown, then cool. Blend a small
jar of inexpensive caviare with the finely chopped whites of
2 hard boiled eggs, 2 tablespoons thick cream, pepper and a
little lemon juice. Put into the pastry cases. Top with sieved
hard boiled egg yolks.
Sardine and cheese boats: Make the boats as above. Prick
well, bake 'blind' until pale golden. Mash sardines with
lemon juice and seasoning to taste. Put into the pastry cases.
Top with grated Gruyère, Cheddar or Parmesan cheese.
Return to the oven for a few minutes to melt the cheese.
Garnish with tomato.
Devilled tuna boats: Make the boats as above. Bake 'blind'
until the pastry has just set; do not over-cook. Meanwhile
open a medium-sized can of tuna, drain away the liquid. Flake
then pound the fish until very smooth with 1 level tablespoon
chutney, 1 teaspoon curry powder and 1 egg. Season well.
Spoon the mixture into the pastry cases, return to the oven
for 6–8 minutes. Garnish with small celery leaves. Serve hot.

Mayonnaise

2 egg yolks
$\frac{1}{2}$–1 teaspoon made mustard
$\frac{1}{4}$–$\frac{1}{2}$ teaspoon salt
shake pepper

pinch sugar
$\frac{1}{4}$ pint ($\frac{2}{3}$ cup) salad or olive oil
1–2 tablespoons vinegar or lemon
  juice

Beat the egg yolks, seasonings and sugar. Very gradually
whisk in the oil and vinegar or lemon juice.

Cheese Aigrettes

1 oz. butter or margarine
3 tablespoons water
2 oz. ($\frac{1}{2}$ cup) flour, preferably
  plain
2 large eggs
1$\frac{1}{2}$ oz. (nearly $\frac{1}{4}$ cup) grated
  Parmesan cheese

seasoning
deep oil for frying
Garnish (optional):
grated Parmesan, or Parmesan and
Cheddar cheese or flaked almonds

Put the butter or margarine with the water into a pan. Heat
until the butter or margarine has melted, remove from the
heat, stir in the flour. Return to the heat and cook gently for
several minutes, until a firm ball. Again remove from the
heat, gradually beat in the eggs until a smooth sticky mixture.
Add the cheese (do not replace over the heat), season well.
Heat the oil to 350°F (until a tiny piece of the mixture turns
golden coloured within about a minute). Drop spoonfuls of the
mixture into the hot oil, lower the heat and cook for about 7
minutes, turning during cooking. Drain well on absorbent
paper and serve on a napkin. Sprinkle with the garnish if
wished.
Makes about 16–20.
Note: These can be fried, put on a flat tray in a low oven and
kept hot for a very limited time only.

Cheese and nut fingers:
Cut fingers of really fresh bread. Coat in cream cheese
moistened with cream or mayonnaise. Roll in chopped nuts.

Sausage Twists

1 lb. small chipolata sausages
puff pastry made with
   4 oz. (1 cup) plain flour etc.
   (see page 20) or 8 oz.
   frozen bought puff pastry

Glaze:
little beaten egg

Grill, fry or bake the sausages for about 6 minutes, until partially cooked. Allow to cool.

Make the pastry (see page 20) and roll out until wafer thin. Cut into strips and roll round the sausages, as shown in the picture on page 118. Put on a baking tray. Brush with beaten egg. Bake for 15 minutes towards the top of a very hot oven, 450–475°F, Gas Mark 7–8. Reduce the heat after 7–8 minutes if necessary. Serve with mustard or one of the sauces below.
Serves 8 as an hors d'oeuvre.

These sauces are all cold, but could be heated in the top of a double saucepan or basin over hot water.

Onion mustard sauce: Blend $\frac{1}{4}$ pint ($\frac{2}{3}$ cup) mayonnaise with 2–3 tablespoons ($\frac{1}{4}$ cup) chopped spring onions or scallions (use the white part only) and 3–4 teaspoons French mustard or use half this quantity of English mustard. Top with the chopped green stems of the spring onions or scallions.

Devilled tomato sauce: Blend $\frac{1}{4}$ pint ($\frac{2}{3}$ cup) mayonnaise with 2 tablespoons tomato purée or ketchup and 2 tablespoons top of the milk or thin cream. Flavour with a few drops chilli and/or Worcestershire sauce. Top with parsley.

Pineapple sweet-sour sauce: Blend $\frac{1}{4}$ pint ($\frac{2}{3}$ cup) mayonnaise with 2–3 tablespoons ($\frac{1}{4}$ cup) syrup from a small can pineapple. Add 2–3 teaspoons vinegar, 1 teaspoon made mustard and the diced pineapple.

Following page: SAUSAGE TWISTS *(Photograph by T. Wall & Son (Meat and Handy Foods) Ltd.)*

Savoury Choux

Pastry:
¼ pint (⅔ cup) water
1 oz. butter or margarine
seasoning
3 oz. (¾ cup) flour, preferably
   plain
2 eggs

1 egg yolk
Fillings:
see below
Garnish:
lettuce
tomato
parsley or unshelled prawns

Put the water and butter or margarine into a pan, season. Heat until the butter or margarine has melted. Remove the pan from the heat, stir in the flour. Return to the heat and cook until a thick ball. Remove once more from the heat, gradually beat in the eggs and the egg yolk, until a smooth mixture. Put teaspoons of the mixture on to well greased baking trays, allowing space for them to rise and spread. If preferred, put into a piping bag with a ¾-inch plain pipe and make the little rounds. Bake for a good 10 minutes, until well risen and firm, above the centre of a hot oven, 425–450°F, Gas Mark 6–7. I like savoury choux slightly browned on the outside; if you do not, then lower the heat slightly. When quite firm remove from the oven, split and remove any slightly under-cooked centre. Return to the oven for 2–3 minutes to dry out. Cool and add the filling.

Serve garnished with lettuce, tomato and parsley or prawns. This makes about 30; allow 3–4 per person.

Fillings for savoury choux:
Mashed well seasoned sardines, or shell-fish in seasoned cream.
Cooked or raw chopped mushrooms in thick seasoned whipped cream.
Grated cheese blended with well seasoned whipped cream, and a few chopped nuts.

Glazed Choux:
Fill the cooked choux buns, brush with a very little egg, sprinkle with grated cheese and return to the oven for a few minutes.

Preceding page: SAVOURY CHOUX

SERVE A DIP

Modern dips or savoury mixtures save a great deal of cooking and preparation. They also help to add to the informal atmosphere of a buffet party, for the bowls of dip, plus the food to serve with the dip, are left on the table and all your guests help themselves.

There are suggestions below and on the following pages for some dips, but you can create your own with little trouble. Make sure the mixture is the consistency of thick cream when blended.

Blend canned crabmeat or salmon with enough mayonnaise and dairy soured cream (or cream and lemon juice) to make a thick cream. Taste and add the flavourings you like, i.e. a little anchovy essence; pinch curry powder; chilli powder; soy sauce.

Blend pâté with a very little mayonnaise, stock and dairy soured cream (or cream and lemon juice). Taste and add flavourings to ensure it is not too bland, i.e. a little made mustard; curry powder; Worcestershire sauce.

Cheeses of all kinds make excellent dips and you can vary the cheese in the recipes on the following pages. If it is a very hard type of cheese you will need to add more liquid.

Commercial dehydrated dips give excellent flavours; make quite sure you leave the mixture to stand for a while, so that the dehydrated ingredients in the packet have time to become moist and mature in flavour.

To serve with dips:

Arrange small biscuits (crackers) of all kinds; potato crisps; small sausages; strips of carrots; pieces of celery; tiny sprigs of raw cauliflower, round the dip. The greater the variety you select, the more interesting the dishes will look.

Sausages with Sour-Sweet Dip

1 lb. cooked, or canned
  frankfurter sausages
Dip:
1 tablespoon made mustard
1 tablespoon vinegar
4 tablespoons tomato ketchup
1 tablespoon honey

1 tablespoon chopped pickled
  onions
1 tablespoon chopped pickled
  walnuts
Garnish:
small onions
gherkins

Arrange the hot or cold sausages round the edge of the dish. Mix the ingredients for the dip together and put into a bowl in the centre of the dish. Spear the onions and gherkins on cocktail sticks and put between the sausages. If using very large sausages halve them.

Variations:
Slice the sausages and put in cream cheese or fingers of other cheese.

Halve bacon rashers; wrap round the sausages, secure with wooden cocktail sticks and cook in the oven until the bacon is crisp. Drain for 1 minute on absorbent paper and serve as above.

Split the sausages and spread with mustard then sandwich the halves together again.

Anchovy Twists: Either bake strips of puff pastry (see page 20) or brush fingers of fresh bread with melted butter and crisp in the oven. Allow to cool, then twist anchovy fillets round these.

Cottage Cheese Dip

1 lb. cottage cheese
$\frac{1}{4}$ pint ($\frac{2}{3}$ cup) soured cream or
  thin cream and 1 tablespoon
  lemon juice
2–3 tablespoons mayonnaise or
  salad dressing

flavouring (see below)
seasoning
Garnish:
paprika or chopped chives

Mix all the ingredients together and season to taste. The cottage cheese can be sieved if wished. Put into a bowl to serve, and top with paprika or chives. Stand on a large dish or tray and arrange a variety of ingredients round it.
Serves 4–6.

To flavour cottage cheese dip:
Crabmeat dip: Open a small can crabmeat or use a small dressed crab. Flake the meat and mix with the basic recipe, add a little extra lemon juice and 2–3 tablespoons finely shredded fresh cucumber.
Curried dip: Blend curry powder, curry paste and a little chutney with the basic recipe. Add a few seedless raisins and grated fresh or desiccated coconut. Leave to stand for a while before serving.
Devilled dip: Blend 2–3 teaspoons made English or French mustard with the ingredients in the basic recipe together with 2–3 tablespoons chopped pickled onions and chopped gherkins and 1–2 teaspoons Worcestershire sauce. To make it hotter, add a few drops chilli sauce.
Herb dip: Blend chopped chives, parsley and crushed garlic with the basic recipe.

Tomato Shrimp Dip

2–3 tablespoons cottage cheese (sieved if wished)
$\frac{1}{2}$ pint (1$\frac{1}{3}$ cups) thick mayonnaise
1–2 tablespoons tomato ketchup or concentrated tomato purée*
2–3 drops chilli sauce

2–3 teaspoons lemon juice
very little finely grated lemon rind
$\frac{1}{2}$–1 teaspoon anchovy essence
about 8 oz. shelled shrimps or chopped shelled prawns

*the former gives a somewhat bland dip, the latter a more 'biting' one.

Mix all the ingredients together.
Serves 8–10.

Savoury Cheese Dip

This is an excellent alternative to tartare sauce. Blend $\frac{1}{4}$ pint ($\frac{2}{3}$ cup) mayonnaise, juice of $\frac{1}{2}$–1 lemon, 4 oz. (1 cup) finely grated Cheddar cheese and $\frac{1}{4}$ pint ($\frac{2}{3}$ cup) thick cream, lightly whipped. Add seasoning and gherkins, parsley and capers as tartare sauce (see page 17).
Serves 5–6.
Other sauces that make good dips are thick tomato sauce, thick curry sauce (page 77) and thick Madeira sauce (page 126).

Avocado Dip (Guacamole)

As Cottage Cheese Dip (page 122), but use 2 mashed avocado pears in place of cottage cheese, flavour with chopped onion and chopped fresh tomatoes.
Serves 4–6.

Salmon Dip

As Cottage Cheese Dip (page 122), but use flaked canned salmon in place of cottage cheese. Flavour with a little chilli sauce, chopped gherkins and capers.
Serves 6–8.

Creamed Chicken Liver Dip

As Cottage Cheese Dip (page 122), but use 1 lb. chickens' livers, cooked in 2 oz. ($\frac{1}{4}$ cup) butter in place of cottage cheese. Sieve, blend with ingredients as Cottage Cheese Dip, flavour with mustard and cream.
Serves 6–8.

Blue Cheese Dip

As Cottage Cheese Dip (page 122), but use half mashed Danish Blue cheese and half cottage cheese.
Serves 6–8.

Cheddar Dip

1½ lb. Cheddar cheese
8 oz. tomatoes

mayonnaise
seasoning

Grate the Cheddar cheese. Skin the tomatoes, sieve or
emulsify and blend with the cheese. Add mayonnaise to give
the consistency of thick cream and season well. Add any
chopped herbs or other flavourings desired.

Miniature Meat Balls

1 lb. cooked meat (either one kind
  or mixture of meats or meat and
  poultry)
2 oz. ($\frac{1}{4}$ cup) butter or margarine
2 oz. ($\frac{1}{2}$ cup) flour
$\frac{1}{2}$ pint (1$\frac{1}{3}$ cups) stock or use half
  stock and half milk
3 oz. (1$\frac{1}{2}$ cups) soft fine bread-
  cumbs or use cheese biscuit
  crumbs

seasoning
2–3 teaspoons chopped fresh
  herbs
1 egg
Coating:
2 eggs
about 3 oz. ($\frac{3}{4}$ cup) crisp
  breadcrumbs
deep cooking fat or oil for frying

Pound the meat until smooth; this makes it easier to form into
balls that do not break when lifted with a cocktail stick.
Make a thick sauce of the butter or margarine, flour and
liquid. Add the meat, crumbs, seasoning, herbs and egg.
Allow the mixture to cool, form into tiny balls. Coat with
beaten eggs then crumbs and fry for just a few minutes.
Drain on absorbent paper. These can be crisped in the hot fat,
then reheated in the oven for a short time, or served cold.
Makes about 40.

Chickens' livers and Bacon

chickens' livers

bacon rashers

Cut the chickens' livers into tiny pieces, wrap in pieces of
bacon and spear with cocktail sticks. Cook for about 10–15
minutes in a moderately hot oven, 375–400°F, Gas Mark 5–6.
If you wish to keep these hot, cover the dish with foil when
the bacon has crisped, and turn the oven to a very low heat.

QUICKIES FOR SUPPER OR BUFFET

Hors d'oeuvres:
Grapefruit cocktails: Open a can of grapefruit segments, drain and chop the fruit and mix with diced canned ham, a little oil, vinegar and seasoning or mix with canned prawns or other fruit.
Melon and ham: Cut slices of melon and arrange on a bed of lettuce with thin slices of canned ham. To serve for a buffet, dice the melon, or make it into balls, cut the ham into neat dice and put a piece of melon and piece of ham on to a cocktail stick. When filled press the sticks into a grapefruit.
Sardine eggs: Hard boil eggs, remove the yolks, mash and mix with mashed sardines, season well and pack back into the white cases. Serve with wedges of lemon on a bed of lettuce or coleslaw.

Main dish:
Barbecued ham: Open a can of ham, put on to an oven-proof dish. Mix equal quantities of tomato juice (canned or fresh), apple juice and Worcestershire sauce. Add a little made mustard. Spoon over the ham and heat in the oven.
Tongue with Madeira sauce: Heat 2 oz. ($\frac{1}{4}$ cup) butter in a pan, stir in 2 oz. ($\frac{1}{2}$ cup) flour and gradually blend in $\frac{1}{2}$ pint ($1\frac{1}{3}$ cups) stock or water and a beef stock cube. Bring to the boil, stir in 1–2 tablespoons red currant jelly and a little made mustard. Heat the canned tongue, slice and serve with the sauce.
For a buffet party make the sauce thicker (like a dip), cut the ham and tongue into small cubes, put on to cocktail sticks and arrange round the dish of sauce.

Desserts
Heat canned or frozen fruit and flavour with brandy, kirsch or other liqueur.

126

Index

PDO 81-652